*Eighteenth Century
French Studies*

Literature and the Arts

Eighteenth Century French Studies

Literature and the Arts

Edited by

E. T. Dubois, Elizabeth Ratcliff, P. J. Yarrow

ORIEL PRESS

© 1969

Bruce Allsopp
A. W. Fairbairn
Edward Lockspeiser
J. Lough
H. T. Mason
R. Niklaus
Francis Scarfe
Christopher Wood

SBN (69UK) 85362 066 0
Library of Congress Card Catalogue Number 70-85810

C

Production Editor, Lucina Hackett
Set in 10 on 12 point Plantin

Published by
ORIEL PRESS LIMITED
27, Ridley Place, Newcastle upon Tyne, NE1 8LH, England

Printed in Scotland by
BELL AND BAIN LIMITED
41-45 Mitchell Street, Glasgow, C.1.

Presented to

Norman Suckling

CONTENTS

CONTENTS

NORMAN CHARLES SUCKLING

Norman Charles Suckling was born at Forest Gate on 24th October 1904. He was educated at Bancroft's School and at Queen's College, Oxford where he graduated in History. He studied at the Metropolitan Academy of Music in London from 1913 to 1921 and in the latter year became a Licentiate of the Royal Academy of Music. In 1925 he was appointed a master at the Liverpool Collegiate School. In 1936 he graduated with First Class Honours in French in the University of London, and in 1943 he was appointed a Lecturer in French at King's College, Newcastle upon Tyne in the University of Durham where he was promoted to the position of Senior Lecturer in 1954. In 1948 he was made Officier d'Académie.

Suckling is both a French scholar and a musician. His compositions include a mass for eight voices, a chamber opera *Avalon*, an introduction and scherzo for string quartet, a sonata in one movement for violin and piano, and a cycle of Shakespeare sonnets for tenor, violin and piano. He is an executant on the piano and with the bassoon. During his years in Liverpool he gave a number of concerts, playing chiefly piano works and chamber music by modern composers. The Sandon Club in that city meant much to him and he meant much to it. His production some thirty-five years ago of *Love's Labour's Lost* with his own incidental music is one of the notable events for which he was responsible, and which are still remembered in the Club where he gave a piano recital as recently as January of this year. During the war of 1939–1945 he gave a series of concerts in the north of England, accompanying various well-known singers. He is specially devoted to French and English music of the late nineteenth and early twentieth centuries and prefers Debussy, Delius, Bax and Ireland to middle-period Beethoven and Schubert. He has contributed a number of papers to such periodicals as the *Monthly Musical Record*, the *Music Review* and *Music and*

Letters. His critical standpoint is shown, for example, in his paper of 1962 in the last-named periodical with the title of 'Tales from the Vienna Backwoods' and in his important and challenging book on Fauré published in 1946.

The depth of Suckling's mind and his outlook on life and literature are shown in his second book entitled *Paul Valéry and the Civilized Mind*, published in 1954 and dedicated to the memory of his first wife who had died five years earlier and had borne him a daughter in 1946. His shrewd judgement of the work of others is to be seen in his many reviews in *Erasmus*.

Suckling's teaching is that of a man who is widely read and has a quick and retentive mind. Generations of pupils are grateful to him, among much else, for the experience of his production of plays by such authors as Giraudoux, Camus, Montherlant, Anouilh, Ionesco and Sartre as well as by Molière, Corneille, Racine and Marivaux. He is admired for his humour and wit, his patience, equanimity and friendliness.

G. B. A. F.

LIST OF PUBLICATIONS BY NORMAN SUCKLING

Books

Fauré, Master Musicians Series, Dent, 1946.
Paul Valéry and the Civilized mind, Oxford University Press for Durham University, 1954.

Articles

'Homage to Gabriel Fauré,' *The Monthly Musical Record*, 1945.
'The Songs of Fauré,' *The Listener*, 1945.
'Gabriel Fauré, Classic of Modern Times,' *The Music Review*, 1945.
' "La Clarté française" in Orchestration,' *Music and Letters*, 1946.
'Vaughan Williams and the Fat Knight,' *The Listener*, 1946.
'Walt Whitman in English Music,' *The Listener*, 1946.
'A further Contribution to the Classic-Romantic Debate,' *Durham University Journal*, 1946.
'Fauré and the Piano,' *The Listener*, 1947.
'The Impact of Vaughan Williams,' *The Listener*, 1947.
'Towards a Better Poetic: the Contribution of the Post-Symbolists,' *French Studies*, 1949.
'Musical Greatness,' *The Monthly Musical Record*, 1948.
'Delius in the Theatre,' *The Listener*, 1948.
'Delius after a Generation,' *The Monthly Musical Record*, 1949.
'The Tragic Symphony,' *The Monthly Musical Record*, 1950.
'What Valéry saw in Pascal,' *Durham University Journal*, 1950.
'Peter Warlock and English Song,' *The Listener*, 1951.
'Delius and the Song of Zarathustra,' *The Listener*, 1951.
'Dryden in Egypt: reflexions on "All for Love",' *Durham University Journal*, 1952.
'The French Revelation,' *The Listener*, 1953.
'John Ireland and the Piano,' *The Listener*, 1953.

'Twenty-five years of English Song,' *The Monthly Musical Record*, 1954.

'Bax and his Piano Sonatas,' *The Listener*, 1954.

'The Sonata in British Piano Music,' *The Listener*, 1955.

'The Neglected Art of Singing,' *The Monthly Musical Record*, 1956.

'The Name and Nature of Love,' *Essays presented to C. M. Girdle-stone*, King's College, Newcastle upon Tyne, 1960.

'Tales from the Vienna Backwoods,' *Music and Letters*, 1962.

'Molière and English Restoration Comedy' in *Stratford-upon-Avon Studies*, No. 6, 1965.

'The enlightenment and the idea of progress,' *Studies on Voltaire and the Eighteenth Century*, LVIII, 1967.

Norman Suckling also has contributed numerous reviews to the *Durham University Journal*, *Erasmus*, *Notes and Queries*, *Music and Letters* and written descriptive notes for gramophone records of French music.

REASON AND SENTIMENT IN EIGHTEENTH-CENTURY ARCHITECTURE

A consideration of essays by Laugier and Boullée

At the beginning of the eighteenth century the Second Church of the Invalides was nearing completion. It had been designed under the imprint of J. H. Mansart and was to become the tomb of Napoleon, a place of secular pilgrimage. Between the building of the dome and the placing under it of the Emperor's blood-red sarcophagus, there was to be a century of prodigious change involving the destruction of many old beliefs and the sacrifice of innumerable lives to hazy concepts of the future. One might expect, if architecture really does mirror society, that there would be pronounced evidences of change in eighteenth-century architecture, but in fact the period begins with the ornamental classicism, which is as near to Baroque as French architecture ever ventured, and closes with a more austere version of the same system of design. The extremes are the chapel of Versailles and the Madeleine. The grammar of classical architecture survived throughout the century and style was refined to a greater degree of academic purity.

One thinks naturally of Versailles, of the great terraced parades laid out by Le Nôtre, of the geometrically-ordered woodlands, the Trianons and the Hamlet. We will return to these; but perhaps the best place of all to reflect upon the strangeness of eighteenth-century architecture in France and begin to understand something of its significance and inner contradictions, is the Place Stanislas at Nancy. One may sip one's aperitif there and, apart from the different dress of people, the motor cars instead of horse-drawn carriages and the slight seediness which pervades a city which has now been engulfed by the French steel industry, but still has an eye to tourism, one might be in the eighteenth century. This delightful setting was built in the middle of the century for the puppet court

❧ I ❧

of an ex-King of Poland, whose daughter, Marie Leczinska, married Louis XV. Here at Nancy, from the Hôtel de Ville, through the triumphal arch and along the *Carrière* to the diminutive palace, one is contained in a deliberately created courtly environment, reflecting the quality and elegance of a ducal entourage which maintained all the apparatus of autocratic government without having any political power. On the left, going up the *Carrière*, the cathedral's ornate spires, designed by J. H. Mansart and G. Boffrand, look discreetly into the precinct without obtruding. The church is just to one side of the composition and is balanced across the way by the beautiful English garden, laid out in romantic style and glimpsed from the *Carrière* through the shining, hand-made glass in the windows of shallow houses which are now mainly lived in by practitioners of law and medicine. Eighteenth-century Nancy is a lovely and precious place, uneasily maintained for it was never quite a reality. It is a survival of a sham and very different from the other seat of the Dukes of Lorraine, at Bar-le-Duc, where the solidly splendid Renaissance houses came into being as part of a long organic development around the real market-place, where the church still dominates the environment and the ducal establishment was behind it. Nancy was the capital of a state without power, and Marie Leczinska was a Queen whose status as a wife endured many humiliations.

In architecture, as in personal relationships, appearances belied reality. This was characteristic of an age of reason which was naïvely unreasonable in its faith in reason. Even Voltaire, legendary philosopher of Ferney and idol of revolutionaries, was a millionaire moneylender and Jean-Jacques Rousseau, apostle of naturalism, lived in urban squalor. The staggering ambiguity of the age is represented at one extreme by Rousseau's well-known confession that he deliberately blamed Madame de Vercelli's maid for stealing a ribbon which he himself had taken. 'Jamais la méchanceté ne fut plus loin de moi que dans ce cruel moment, et lorsque je chargeai cette malheureuse fille, il est bizarre, mais il est vrai que mon amitié pour elle en fut la cause. Elle étoit présente à ma pensée, je m'excusai sur le premier objet qui s'offrit.' At the other extreme we have Père Laugier of the Society of Jesus preaching in the sumptuous chapel of Versailles to the royal family against the sinful ways of Louis XV. This was in Lent 1754 and it was only when he had seemingly sided with the Parlement one Sunday, in preaching of the duties of kingship, and demanded the extinction of the Parlement as the destroyer of religion on the next Sunday, that he was encouraged to leave Paris for a time. Both these equivocal men influenced architectural thought, but the waves of feeling and the tides of fashion for sentiment and sensibility washed round the fluted columns of the Orders of Architecture and subsided leaving them as strong as ever. They may well be seen as a monument to what was reasonable in the age of reason, but even here there is paradox because the logic of the Orders is internal to a system of thought about architecture which may well be judged arbitrary and demands acceptance as an act of faith. Much of the argument which went on in the salons of Paris led in a circle, back to the justification of old rules by new reasons. The more architectural theory changed, the more it remained the same. This, however, was not limited to the eighteenth century. Alberti had poured scorn upon Vitruvius as being an illiterate workman, but reiterated his doctrine in Ciceronian Latin; and a comparison of Alberti with the modern theoretical writings of Le Corbusier discloses a remarkable degree of similarity.

To understand the enduring correctness of eighteenth-century architecture one must look back to its origins. To any serious student of architectural invention and achievement outside France, Mansart must mean François and not his sister's grandson Jules Hardouin, who adopted his august name. From Le Breton, the master craftsman of Fontainebleau who impressed France upon the Italian way of designing buildings, through Primaticcio, the talented Italian who gave classical validity to alien genius in the Aile de la Belle Cheminée, to Philibert de l'Orme, who asserted, in his book *L'Architecture* in 1567, French superiority over the Italian aesthetic and so to de Brosse and François Mansart, the French had taken the Renaissance way of design to themselves and transformed it.

Before François all was a projection, an adaptation, even a vulgarization of Italian achievement, but with Mansart Renaissance architecture acquired a new quality.

Maisons-Lafitte, perhaps his greatest work, is now a place on the commuter line to St. Lazare and the grandeur of the château is assaulted by speculative housing; its gardens are ruthlessly despoiled. Yet in Maisons the French version of Renaissance architecture had been achieved: Versailles and the Second Church of the Invalides were then all but inevitable.

A Fantasy by Meissonnier

The reign of Louis XIV is marked in architecture by the career of Colbert and official recognition of the value of architecture in promoting the prestige of France. The Académie became both the channel for patronage and the means of ensuring that, whatever might go on inside the buildings and in the minds of men and women, the outward image would remain dignified, respectable and essentially French. Under the influence of the Académie the work begun by Philibert de l'Orme in developing a French aesthetic was carried on and a formidable body of theoretical writing was compiled.

It is true that there was a dissident element, mostly either originating outside France or finding its opportunities abroad. For example, the fantasies of J. A. Meissonnier were created mainly for export and he was himself a native of Turin. Oppenordt's extravagances were of Dutch ancestry and imbued with a spirit of late Baroque in Italy where he spent several years. The great masters of French decoration were often extravagant: there was architectural virtue in being expensive at the court of the Sun King but they kept within the accepted bounds of ponderous classical taste and for this mixed blessing one must look to the overriding influence of Le Brun who was virtually an artistic dictator. The pomposity of Le Brun's work is always based upon a regular formal geometry but, with the rococo, interior designers, who came increasingly into fashion during the early eighteenth century, symmetry was deliberately broken down. They had to work within the structural symmetry of the buildings, but in panels, mirrors, arabesques, furnishings of all kinds, like Italian mannerists of the sixteenth century, but for different reasons, they seem to have delighted in rejecting reasonable order. Yet it was without any strong tinge of personal expressionism such as we find in Giulio Romano and to a much greater extent in the work of German artists.

The reason for this may be sought in the peculiar innovation of salon society, originated, it is said, in the seventeenth century by the Marquise de Rambouillet, Catherine de Vivonne. This system, in which the aristocracy mingled on terms of equality with men of letters and in which women had a dominant role, gave enormous social and political importance to polite conversation and to the cultivation of the art of mixing with people, to the necessity for *l'air galant* which Mademoiselle de Scudéry described as being a favourable natural disposition, a knowledge of the world and a desire to please without loving anybody special. In the atmosphere of the salon and under the influence of that growing scepticism which is most commonly associated with Voltaire, any kind of stolidity or moralism was anathema, and the rococo style of interior design seems to have provided the perfect background for that unreasonable and coquettish elegance which permeated polite society in rooms behind the bland façades of Nancy, Paris or Versailles.

One purpose of books is to nourish the conversation of people who must talk but could not possibly think for themselves, and at a time when the output of publishers was not only limited by paucity of manuscripts but also by official censorship, the advent of a highly controversial book on architecture was a boon. It was written by Marc-Antoine Laugier, a Jesuit, and approved by the censor at the end of November 1752. Its title was *Essai sur l'Architecture* and it set out to tell architects the error of their ways and lay down the rules by which they ought to design. Optimistically he wrote, 'Je me persuade que ceux de nos Architectes qui ont un véritable zele pour la perfection de leur Art, me sçauront gré de ma bonne volonté,' and hoped they would not reject the light out of antipathy to the source from whence it came. He thought of himself as a philosopher and in a later work—quoted below—he maintained that it was the prerogative of philosophers to instruct artists in the rules of their art. Laugier was not a philosopher, except in his own conceit, but he was a forerunner of the modern art critic. He was a man of considerable education and intellect who had a genuine interest in and concern for the art of architecture to which he applied himself with all the apparatus of the Jesuit dialectic. Characteristically he began with a statement of belief which he then proceeded to justify.

Essai sur l'Architecture had most of the qualities of a natural best-seller. Its author had no practical knowledge of the subject, upon which he wrote with the naïve confidence of ignorance. It was written with the easy stylishness of a *prédicateur du Roi*. It appealed to the authority of antiquity, for the Orders of Architecture, but it also went 'back to the source' and found the essentials of architectural theory in simple nature, in the 'rustic hut' which the primitive man—akin to the noble savage—built to provide shelter in an idyllic landscape. Such deference to nature, no matter how misleading, doffed the cap in passing to the august figure of Sir Isaac Newton at the same time as smiling towards the sentimental naturalism of Rousseau. It beguilingly resolved the essential aesthetic

conflict of the age between the idea that beauty is inherent in and consequent upon the observance of divine laws, as Alberti had believed, and the view expressed by Dubos that the distinction between what is good and bad in art lies not in reason but in *sentiment*. Consensus of cultivated opinion (cf. David Hume), it was widely believed, confirmed the validity of the old laws even though Newtonian science, and religious scepticism, had demolished their original foundations. But perhaps Laugier's most endearing quality to his salon admirers and discussants was his establishment of the authority of the amateur over the artist which was to wreak such havoc with the lives of the most talented artists in France during the next hundred and fifty years. In the preface to the second edition (1765) he said explicitly that his principal design was to form the taste of architects: 'Comme mon principal dessein est de former le goût des Architectes ...'

Laugier appealed to the most profitable, indeed the only possible audience for such a work and it is not surprising that the architects of his time reacted strongly against him. Not only was he asserting the authority of the philosopher over the artist but he was propounding a doctrine which appealed to the non-practising reader as simple and natural, and astounded the practical architect by its total impracticability.

To substantiate this statement we must look to the actual content of *Essai sur l'Architecture*. Much of the essay is entirely conventional but it is enlightened by some ideas about town planning which deserve to be noticed and an awareness of the beauties of Gothic architecture which is remarkable in France at that time, though it would have been commonplace in England where Walpole was already building Strawberry Hill. Voltaire considered Notre Dame in Paris to be a mixture of filigree and barbarism but Laugier, while admitting it is not the best in France, is struck by the extent, the height, *le dégagement* and praises it above 'modern work'. The seminal part of Laugier's essay is the beginning in which he enunciates the dogma that the elements of 'la petite cabane rustique' are the essentials of architecture. 'I therefore come to this conclusion' he says, 'in every architectural order only the column, the entablature and the pediment could form an essential part of its composition. If each of these three parts is suitably placed and suitably formed nothing else need be added to make the work perfect.'

But it has to be admitted that functional requirements may modify this ideal arrangement and they are admitted because they are practically indispensable. They are described as *licences* and included not only doors and windows but architectural devices which had been used by great architects in the past, such as broken pediments. Even walls were a *licence*! The 'rustic hut' had four posts and a roof but people require privacy so walls are allowed as a *licence*! Laugier was propounding a pure post and lintel architecture and, though he did not say so, Stonehenge might perhaps be taken as its perfect embodiment. Even the Parthenon had the *licence* of the cella walls. The less wall the better 'et s'il n'en paroît rien du tout, l'ouvrage sera parfait', he maintained. And apart from details sanctioned by the authority of great architects, and functional necessities such as doors, windows and walls, most other embellishments were abuses denounced under the term of *caprices* which must not occur in architecture. What an astounding contradiction of the fashionable interiors of the time! Among the abuses are niches, arcades and pilasters which are 'the bastard child of architecture' because they are 'the faulty imitation of a beautiful original'.

Laugier's essay teems with contradictions and outrageous deductions. It attempted to reduce the most complicated and difficult of all artistic disciplines to a simple formula of three components. It was ineffably naïve and yet it was influential. It involved the public, or rather that section of the public which thought that talking about art was important, in the criticism of architecture and there were several peculiar fruits from this. One was the development of informed public opinion about architecture and it must be said that Laugier's essay took its place in the stream of non-academic art criticism which probably began with the critical review of the *Salon* of 1747 by La Font de Sainte-Yenne. The result was an envenomed battle between men of letters and artists which

B*

has continued to the present day though in somewhat muted forms. The essence of the controversy is contained in Laugier's statement, in the preface to his later book *Observations sur l'Architecture* (1765):

C'est aux Philosophes à porter le flambeau de la raison dans l'obscurité des principes et des régles. L'exécution est le propre de l'Artiste, et c'est au Philosophe qu'appartient la législation.

This is a claim which artists are bound to contest but the architect is in a special relationship to his client, to the public and to criticism because his work always involves the expenditure of large sums of money and consequently professional responsibility devolves upon him. He is not, like the painter or sculptor, a prime maker but a designer whose buildings are accomplished through the agency of a contractor and many workmen. In eighteenth-century France the architect was already a professional man depending for patronage upon his conformity with the aims of the Académie. There is something of the vicar of Bray in most professional men and they are remarkably impotent in influencing their professional future. Indeed, there is an element of implied obligation to serve in the nature of professionalism, as well as a certain timidity fostered by membership of a closed shop and the security it provides, which makes professional men peculiarly susceptible to change imposed from outside. Architects feel that they must adapt or perish and on the few occasions when they have, as a group, gone against the tide, they have been replaced by more compliant people, as happened to the master-mason architects at the time of the Renaissance. Something similar is happening now. It is not necessarily good but the current public attitude—sentiment if you like—seems to make it inevitable.

The academicians of France in the time of Laugier were inclined to concede in matters of decoration and uphold the rules of classical art in building. Decoration was ephemeral, like fashions in dress, but architecture was permanent or at least long-enduring. Laugier's theories did not conflict with this view but introduced two new ideas which, though initially resisted, were assimilated. The first was a puritanical doctrine of cultivating primal simplicity:

the second and related doctrine was that this simplicity was 'natural' and therefore good. Neither doctrine was original but there was a degree of innovation in applying them to architecture, and thus Laugier may be judged to have been the means by which architects were led to an adjustment which brought them into line with current sentiment. But in spite of this the dialectic of the Académie enabled them to achieve adjustment by a refinement of their first principles! The Panthéon (Sainte Geneviève) and the Madeleine mark the path they followed, and the Madeleine is the apotheosis of the little rustic hut.

Ten years after the writing of Laugier's *Essai* J. A. Gabriel designed the Petit Trianon. It is a Palladian villa of modest size and owes nothing to Laugier. Indeed in the detailing of the exterior there are a number of elegant deviations from strict classical rules as, for example, in the weathering over the ground floor windows and the lower balustrading, not to mention the abuse of pilasters. Royalty was escaping from the oppressive grandeur of the palace to a habitation of human scale but this was still formal and classical in design. The next stage was the nostalgic naturalism of the Hamlet, utterly charming in its playful design and pathetic in its significance. Like architecture, French royalty maintained its façade and lost touch with reality; and just as the architects conceded interior decoration and garden design to rococo and romance, so royalty compromised with a sentimental make-believe of rustic simplicity. Here was the rustic hut again, not in the context of architectural theory but as an expression of the communal illusion of the age, that primitive simplicity was not only good and beautiful but relevant to the problems of a distraught society.

At the opposite extreme to the Hamlet at Versailles there is the architecturally more significant work of Etienne-Louis Boullée (1728–1799) who also wrote an essay entitled *Architecture, Essai sur l'Art* which was not published and went with his papers to the Bibliothèque Nationale. It had no direct influence but it is a fascinating cocoon of thought about architecture in the last quarter of the eighteenth century. Boullée was a pleasant, happy and paternal bachelor who inspired the affection of many young architects, but as a designer his best work went into the creation of colossal fantasies presented in magnificent drawings which, as Dr. Rosenau has suggested, 'largely took the place of executed design, since for him it was vision which counted'.

Here was a different kind of escape into a megalomaniac dream world where architecture was free from the embarrassments of firmness and commodity. Among his schemes there is a Cenotaph for Newton comprising a vast sphere four-hundred-and-twenty feet in diameter resting on a plinth of stone, like an egg in an egg-cup and functioning as a planetarium. There is a Chapel to the Dead on an even grander scale and a more realistic design for the Bibliothèque Nationale with nude Atlas figures, twenty-five feet tall, supporting a globe over the portal. His detailed project for an Opera House surpasses anything Utzen proposed for Sydney and includes enormous pointed vaults within a hemispherical dome. But it must not be thought that these were un-architectural fantasies. They did in fact represent an extension of Boullée's philosophy towards the realization of an ideal architecture unfettered by practicalities. There is nothing of Gustave Doré, Piranesi or John Martin about these designs. They are pure intellectual exercises in architecture and conform to Boullée's belief that architecture is divided into 'l'art proprement dit et la science'. 'Il faut concevoir pour effectuer', he says and it was with conception that he was principally concerned. This was just as well for him because the revolutionary period afforded little opportunity for an architect to build.

The mood of Boullée's essay is calm and gracious, and he has one great advantage over Laugier: he spoke from experience of what it means to create architecture. Was he merely the mirror of his age with his escapades into gigantic abstractions and his belief that natural laws of mass and proportion were the foundation of the art of architecture; or was he more than that? His essay remained unpublished until 1952 but he seems to have been a sociable man, a professor at the *Écoles Centrales*, an academician from 1762 and a member of the *Institut*. What he wrote in his essay he no doubt discussed with friends and students. Read then this paragraph and think of the Opera in Paris:

A l'imitation de la nature, l'art de rendre les grandes images en architecture, consiste à disposer les corps qui forment l'ensemble général, de manière qu'ils ayent beaucoup de jeu, que leurs masses aient un mouvement noble, majestueux, et qu'elles soient susceptibles du plus grand développement. Dans l'ensemble, l'ordre des choses doit être combiné tellement que nous puissions d'un coup d'œil, embrasser la multiplicité des objets qui le composent. Il faut que la lumière, en se répandant sur la réunion des corps, y produise les effets les plus étendus, les plus frappans, les plus variés et les plus multipliés. Dans un grand tout, les parties accessoires, combinées avec art, doivent donner à l'ensemble la plus grande richesse; et c'est cette richesse heureusement répartie, qui produit la pompe et la magnificence.

La magnificence! Despite all the horrors of revolution, indeed perhaps because of them, the Michelangelesque dream of the splendour of man must be revived. Splendour, Glory, Magnificence; men died in their thousands and Napoleon was entombed under the Dome of the Invalides.

Boullée was influenced by the common sentiment of the age but he saw his mission as the expression of this sentiment in terms of architecture and herein he looks towards the century which began a year after his death. Sixty years later the Paris Opera comes very near to the realization of Boullée's intellectual fantasies. But the most surprising element in Boullée's thinking is his separation of art and science referred to above. Here he went, as he acknowledged, against the teaching of Vitruvius and most previous theorists. 'La définirai-je avec Vitruve, l'art de bâtir? Non. Il y a dans cette définition, une erreur grossière. Vitruve prend l'effet pour la cause.' 'Most authors,' he says, 'have concerned themselves with the scientific side of architecture . . . but not a single one of these authors has any idea of the constituent principles of their art.' Boullée distinguishes himself as one who is concerned with *art as such* and herein we find an astonishing anticipation of that belief in art for its own sake which was to culminate in *L'Art Nouveau* at the end of the nineteenth century. The separation of the science of building from the art of architecture was a dangerous one but it made possible a new discipline of architecture which was developed by the Académie and, through the École des Beaux-Arts, established Paris as the centre for architectural education based upon an intellectual system of design.

En un mot, le compas de la raison ne doit jamais abandonner le génie de l'architecte qui doit toujours prendre, pour règle, cette belle maxime: 'Rien de beau si tout n'est sage.'

Sage is a word of many meanings but it seems clear that Boullée, at the end of the century, was convinced of the virtue of reason in architecture and this was the pattern of the future in France no matter how strange some of the reasoning.

For the 'civilized mind' there is no need to justify the study of history. It is more than 'le tableau des crimes et des malheurs' and an age of schism such as our own may well profit from a study of the paradoxes of eighteenth-century thought and feeling. We might even avoid the logical conclusion.

REFERENCES

The primary sources of this study are two essays on architectural theory; *Essai sur l'Architecture* by Marc-Antoine Laugier first published in Paris in 1753 and *Architecture, Essai sur l'Art* by Etienne-Louis Boullée written in the last years of the eighteenth century. The former is available in the Gregg Press facsimile of the second edition (1755); the latter forms part of Ms 9153 in the Bibliothèque Nationale and was first published in 1952 by Tiranti, London, with a preface and notes by Dr. Helen Rosenau. I have also used Wolfgang Herrmann's *Laugier and Eighteenth Century Theory* published in London by Zwemmer in 1962. This excellent study provides extensive appendices of source material covering the principal contributors to aesthetic thought in the first half of the eighteenth century. But for any study of the visual arts literary sources are only part of the evidence: the actual buildings of the eighteenth century must be seen and experienced if their significance is to be understood. Laugier would have agreed with this: he was, within his blinkers, a most sensitive observer of architecture. I am not so sure about Boullée: he had architecture in his head.

The picture on page 7 is the frontispiece to Laugier's *Essai* and visualizes the 'rustic hut'.

BRUCE ALLSOPP

PIERRE BAYLE AND THE CHEVALIER RAMSAY

Although the Chevalier Andrew Michael Ramsay[1] early repudiated Calvinism, it was not until after a period of spiritual and intellectual discontent that he was definitively confirmed in the kind of inward religion which he imbibed from the George Garden group in Scotland, from Pierre Poiret in Holland, and from Fénelon and Madame Guyon in France. Nevertheless, his eclectic pursuit of truth during this period became the groundwork of his not inconsiderable attainments as a philosopher. By studying diligently and meditating, as well as by seeking counsel, he attained to certitude, though not without coming under the tutelage of several very dissimilar thinkers, both English and French.

Among these, as Ramsay himself has attested, was Pierre Bayle. In outlining the contributions of his chief mentors in the *Lettre de M. Ramsay à M. de la Motte sur la religion*,[2] he describes himself as having been in turn the disciple of Newton, Bayle, Fénelon, and Malebranche. His particular debt to Bayle, here termed 'ce Démocrite français' (an allusion to Bayle's varied learning and wide influence as well as to the Greek philosopher's attempt to explain colour), consists of the theory that extension may resemble colour in being a purely sensible quality with no external reality. The basis for Ramsay's extreme satisfaction with this notion, which in Bayle's *Dictionnaire historique et critique*[3] is outlined in remark B of the article Pyrrhon and expounded in remark G of the article Zénon d'Elée, derives from its harmony with his increasingly quietistic leanings. It is perhaps this temperamental factor which also explains his apparent indifference to the fact that Bayle was not sponsoring such an idea *in propria persona* but merely instancing certain sceptical argumentations, notably a neo-Zenonian paradox which impugned the belief in motion by predicating that extension did not have objective existence. Moreover, in the article Zénon,

Bayle added a rider or caveat indicating that, despite the philosophical difficulties involved in the movement of extended substances, '[il] ne laisse pas de suivre l'opinion commune'.[4]

In addition to having so readily assimilated one of the more bizarre notions to find expression in the *Dictionnaire*, it is likely that Ramsay was also acquainted with Bayle's *Avis aux Réfugiés*. This, Cherel[5] regards as one of the sources of Ramsay's *Essai sur le gouvernement civil*,[6] and important similarities of argument suggest the correctness of his judgement. Both works refute the doctrine of the sovereignty of the people;[7] and both point out that what pass for popular political movements are always brought about by interested minorities which have no mandate from the nation at large.[8]

However, that Ramsay could credit Bayle with an important rôle in his intellectual formation is not easily deducible from the Chevalier's writing as sa whole. On the contrary, in his *Discours sur la mythologie des païens*—a supplement to his most famous work, *Les Voyages de Cyrus*[9]—Bayle is expressly attacked, initially on the seemingly negligible count of having imputed dualism to the Magi.[10] Since this allegation conflicted with one of the assumptions underlying *Les Voyages de Cyrus*, namely that the philosophers of all ages and countries had recognized a supreme Deity, Ramsay obviously deemed it expedient to conclude his demonstration of the essential monotheism of the ancient Persians by contradicting so disseminated a reference-book as the *Dictionnaire*; and he improved the occasion by proceeding to disparage its author in more general fashion:

M. Bayle dit dans son Dictionnaire que les anciens Perses étaient tous manichéens. Il aurait sans doute abandonné ce sentiment s'il avait consulté les auteurs originaux. C'est ce que ce célèbre critique ne faisait pas toujours. Il avait un génie capable de tout approfondir; mais il écrivait quelquefois à la hâte et se contentait d'effleurer les matières les plus graves. D'ailleurs on ne peut justifier cet auteur d'avoir trop aimé l'obscurité désolante du pyrrhonisme. Il semble dans ses ouvrages être toujours en garde contre les idées satisfaisantes sur la religion. Il montre avec art et subtilité tous les côtés obscurs d'une question; mais il en présente rarement le point lumineux d'où sort l'évidence. Quels éloges n'eût-il pas mérité s'il avait employé ses rares talents plus utilement pour le genre humain![11]

The gravamen of this long complaint against Bayle was not of course the comparative peccadillo of defective scholarship, but his liking for raising difficulties when treating matters of religion: a tendency manifestly abhorrent to Ramsay, whose major writings are not only apologetic in aim but reveal a fastidious concern with the methods of rational persuasion. Hence, in his work *Les Voyages de Cyrus*, which describes the educational, political, and religious formation of a perfect ruler, that contrived gradualness by which Ramsay guides his hero—and, he doubtless hoped, his readers—from atheism to deism, from deism to Socinianism, and from Socinianism to Christianity. Similarly, that technique of reiteration which is used to make manifest the former universality of his own fondly held belief in three states of human existence: a pristine purity and felicity from which man has fallen; a present condition of degradation and sin subserving a redemptive and retributive purpose; and a restored innocence and bliss. This is the key feature of the instruction given to Cyrus by, respectively, Zoroastre (Book II), Sonchis (Book III), Pythagore (Book VI), Eléazar (Book VIII), and Daniel (Book VIII).

Neatly interpolated into the *Discours sur la mythologie*, Ramsay's reproof of Bayle appears to have been intended to contribute to its underpinning of the delicate theological structure erected around the travels of Cyrus. Since Ramsay cannot have been unaware of the effect produced by the Manichean articles of the *Dictionnaire*, it is probable that the theodicy embodied in *Les Voyages de Cyrus* was in part inspired by the debate which they had initiated. Certainly Ramsay's depiction of evil as being the chief impediment to Cyrus's advance in faith was both topical and realistic. In disputing with Anaximandre, who resembles Bayle by combining Pyrrhonism with a polemical insistence on the problem of evil, the orthodox Pythagore, though triumphing in other respects, leaves unanswered objections which, both in substance and in formulation, are markedly akin to some of those raised in remark D of the article Manichéens.[12] Not surprisingly, Cyrus later interrogates the more percipient Eléazar about what he introduces as this 'grande difficulté que nul philosophe n'a pu me résoudre'. Nor does the reply that liberty is an inevitable concomitant of man's creation as an intelligent being go far to satisfy him. Only when Eléazar points to the relation between finiteness and fallibility—a suggestion reminiscent of one of the main contentions made in Part I of the *Théodicée* by the greatest of Bayle's opponents, Leibniz, whom Ramsay mentions in the *Discours sur la mythologie*[13]—will he accept that moral evil derives, not from the Divinity, 'mais de la faiblesse inséparable de notre nature bornée, qui peut se tromper et s'égarer'. Even so, Cyrus presses for a specific explanation of physical evil; and not until after Eléazar has interpreted it as the necessary cure for moral evil, in that suffering is the sole remedy for sin, does he come to recognize that God 'ne châtie que pour corriger. Il ne punit que pour guérir'.

Although Ramsay found much to gratify him in the reception of *Les Voyages de Cyrus* as a prose romance, its praise as such was in at least one instance more than offset by the gravest gainsaying of its value as a defence of Christianity. After deploring its syncretism, which was likened to that of Pierre-Daniel Huet, the *Lettre du père Vinot de l'Oratoire à Madame la comtesse d'Agénois, sur la Cyropoédie de M. de Ramsay*[14] crisply exposed the major flaw in its theology by pointing out that the concept of the 'trois états du monde', implying as it did the soul's pre-existence and premundane fall, was supposititious and therefore valueless as a solution of the origin of evil. Furthermore, the prophet Daniel's heretical acquiescence in these beliefs left Cyrus with the illusion that there was little or no difference between this ternary existential system of his pagan teachers and the truth revealed in the sacred scriptures. And as an *obiter dictum* Vinot added: 'je crois, dans le fond, M. de Ramsay amateur de cet âge éternel de nos âmes; il semble avoir regret à la condamnation d'Origène.'

Ramsay's earnestness in defending what he considered to be true religion—it has been justly said that he scarcely deserves the pejorative appellation *un aventurier religieux*[15]—prompted him to undertake an apologia, posthumously published as *Lettre de M. de Ramsay à Madame la comtesse d'Agénois, à l'occasion de la Lettre critique du père Vinot, qui lui avait été communiquée.*[16] In it he stated that he had sought, not to dogmatize Origen's hypotheses of the pre-existence and ultimate restoration of souls, but, through the person of Eléazar, to show their cogency in a philosophical refutation of the difficulties concerning the origin of evil, including those raised by Bayle. In this connection—and here Ramsay's theological presuppositions lead to an interesting and unusual stricture upon the *Dictionnaire*—he went on to denounce what he termed the work's sophistic use of revealed religion as the source of objections against natural religion. To counter this move, he argued that the realms of reason and faith should be rigorously defined, so as to stress that such doctrines as original sin and external punishment were revealed religious dogmas, which reason alone did not inculcate. Having appositely interposed this assessment of Bayle's religious criticism, Ramsay continued his self-defence by explaining that, since the Origenistic tenets in question had once been permitted and were consistent with reason, he had adduced them to support the appeal to faith which he was making through an *argumentum a fortiori*. For if the weak and finite reason of the philosophers could conceive a solution to the enigma of evil, did it not follow that 'Dieu peut trouver, dans sa raison infinie, de quoi justifier un jour les démarches incompréhensibles de sa providence'? Moreover, the juxtaposition of the rationalizing Eléazar and the inspired Daniel, whose authoritative utterances form the climax of Cyrus's religious quest, brought home the very needful lesson that, in the last analysis, philosophical speculation was a vain endeavour which must give place to a humble trust in the unfathomable but sure outworking of the divine purpose.

Despite this reassuring tone, in part due to a conciliatory temperament enhanced by the special circumstance that he was replying through a respected intermediary to a courteous stranger who had not withstood him openly, neither the revised edition of *Les Voyages de Cyrus* (1730) nor Ramsay's subsequent theological lucubrations were to exhibit the sedate orthodoxy which Vinot palpably required of him. Yet although the Chevalier was to remain an almost opinionatedly eccentric apologist, what is not in doubt is the sincerity of his censure of the *Dictionnaire*, which reinforces what he had already written about Bayle in the *Discours sur la mythologie*. Taken together, they establish that Bayle's Manichean arguments were much in Ramsay's mind at the time of his composition of *Les Voyages de Cyrus*; and it also emerges that, certainly in retrospect and perhaps in prospect, he envisaged Book VIII, which concludes the work by contrasting the *ne plus ultra* of the human intellect with the God-givenness of saving belief, as a corrective to Bayle's bedevilling treatment of the relation between reason and faith. It should be added that Ramsay might have been less sanguine about his success in this regard had he known, or borne in mind, that Jean Le Clerc, who had likewise opposed Bayle in the guise of an Origenist in *Parrhasiana* (1699), had been easily worsted in their ensuing controversy.

Meanwhile, Ramsay's hostile comments on Bayle were themselves the subject of adverse criticism on the part of at least two distinguished readers of *Les Voyages de Cyrus*, of whom one, Mathieu Marais, probably Bayle's greatest admirer in France, reacted with predictable asperity and sarcasm. Obviously with the latter's *Eclaircissements* principally in mind, Marais, in a letter to the Academician Jean Bouhier dated 17 December 1727,[17] maintained that Bayle had exculpated himself in advance of all the charges brought against him; and his having impelled Leibniz to undertake the rebutting *Théodicée* made nonsense of the charge of superficiality. In fact, 'c'est bien ce M. de Ramsay qui n'est qu'un *effleureur*'. As for Ramsay's merits as an author: 'L'article de *Zoroastre* de Bayle vaut mieux que tout son livre ...'

Writing from Dijon on 22 December, Bouhier urbanely replied: 'Le Cyrus de Ramsay n'a point encore voyagé jusqu'ici.'

Like his friend and correspondent, whose low estimate of the work he was inclined to accept, Bouhier ridiculed Ramsay's depreciation of Bayle as a thinker, which Marais had concisely summarized. With much pertinency, Bouhier was able to cite a recent testimony to the contrary by the noted Jesuit René-Joseph Tournemine:

Pour ce qui est de Bayle, il est absurde de dire qu'il ne fait qu'effleurer les matières, surtout celles de religion et de métaphysique. Il ne les enfonce que trop et je me souviens d'avoir ouï dire cet été au P. de Tournemine, qui travaille à une réfutation des athées, qu'il ne trouvait rien de plus difficile à résoudre que certaines objections proposées par votre ami et que je suis sûr que Ramsay n'entend seulement pas. Je ne sais même si feu M. de Cambrai son maître les entendait bien aussi. Car vous savez que les raisonnements philosophiques n'étaient pas son fort. Quoiqu'il en soit, il faudra pourtant voir Cyrus, comme on a vu Gulliver. Car on jetterait la pierre à quelqu'un qui ne l'aurait pas lu.[18]

In their next exchange of letters, Marais and Bouhier continued this reciprocation of concurring judgements at Ramsay's expense. On 23 December 1727, Marais, who had just reread the articles Manichéens, Marcionites, Pauliciens, Zoroastre, and the *Eclaircissement sur les Manichéens*, vigorously added to his litany of fulminations against Bayle's impudent critic.[19] A week later, on 30 December, Bouhier, who had at length received a copy of *Les Voyages de Cyrus*, referred scathingly to Ramsay's attitude to 'un aussi grand métaphysicien que Bayle, dont il n'est pas digne de déchausser les souliers'.[20] His remarks on the work itself were couched in similarly scornful language.

In view of Bouhier's conviction, expressed in his letter to Marais of 2 November 1734, that the *Mémoires de Trévoux* had sunk almost to the level of the *Mercure*,[21] it would be interesting to have had his opinion of an article which appeared in the Jesuits' journal in April of the following year under the heading *Le Psychomètre ou réflexions sur les différents caractères de l'esprit, par un milord anglais*.[22] This is recognizably by Ramsay, to whom it was indeed attributed on its republication in Descevole's *Ambigu littéraire* of 1782. As well as affording an insight into Ramsay's literary and intellectual culture, this work reveals him to have possessed some ability as a critic, here exercised in classifying great men in terms which primarily denote the shapes and properties of material things. Brief though this essay is, Bayle has a conspicuous place in it. In company with Pico della Mirandola, Leibniz, Boerhaave, Fontenelle, and Tournemine, he is described as broad; and in the series of parallels to which this kind of basic categorization leads, that between Henry More and Spinoza concludes with the assertion that the English philosopher's Origenistic conception of the universe meets all Bayle's queries respecting the origin and continuance of evil. In praising More in this way, Ramsay discloses his continuing sympathy with this world-view and the probable inspiration of the argument, in *Les Voyages de Cyrus*, to which Vinot had taken such exception.[23] *Le Psychomètre* ends with a comparison between Bayle and Fontenelle, who are stated to be alike in their universality, though 'le dernier paraît avoir un génie bien plus profond et plus exact que le premier'. Continuing in this vein of mingled esteem and blame, Ramsay avowed Bayle's immense erudition in the fields of history, metaphysics, and the humanities before renewing, in places almost verbatim, the severe criticism of the latter which he had earlier made in the *Discours sur la mythologie*.

Ramsay's remaining years, before his death at the age of about fifty-seven in 1743, were principally devoted to what became his *opus magnum*, an elaborate two-volumed defence of Christianity which his friends the Foulis brothers published at Glasgow in 1748–1749 as *The Philosophical Principles of Natural and Revealed Religion. Unfolded in a Geometrical Order by the Chevalier Ramsay, Author of the Travels of Cyrus.* As in so many other early eighteenth-century works of an apologetic nature, among them Ramsay's own best-seller, which was now available in several French and English editions, Bayle received a full measure of obloquy. Ramsay's methodological exordium, which explains the ground of his semi-mathematical 'organon' is typical in this respect. After asserting that there are two forms of metaphysics—that of scholasticism and an authentic sort whose inductions and deductions have order, clarity, and precision—he underscored this contention by claiming that those who accept geometry as the only demonstrable science 'must naturally fall into a sceptical indolence, maintain that Pyrrho and Bayle have wrote [sic] the true history of the human mind, and that all other philosophers have only given the romance of it'.[24] Bayle's scepticism is opposed, too, in Ramsay's development of the system of logic that had been tersely embodied in a footnote to *Les Voyages de Cyrus*,[25] where Pyrrhonism was said to issue from the error of not distinguishing between demonstration (which implies that the contrary is impossible), proof (where there is every reason to believe and none to doubt), and probability (where there is greater reason to believe than to doubt). In the *Philosophical Principles*, a homily on the dangers of confusing these three kinds of evidence singles out Bayle as an arch-exponent of this vice of reasoning, in that 'to throw the mind into an universal scepticism, he shows that demonstrations cannot be given where only proofs are requisite; and to invalidate the force of proofs he insinuates that they are not demonstrations'.[26] This preludes an assailment of Bayle which continues in much the same terms as in the *Discours sur la mythologie* and *Le Psychomètre*.

Ramsay's 'Great Work' on religion predictably impugns Bayle on issues other than that of the nature of knowledge and the science of reasoning. In his consideration of the attributes of God, which occupies Books I and II, the Proposition that 'Absolute infinite excludes all duality and plurality of substance' has a scholium with five corollaries, the last of which is specifically directed against Bayle's Manichean arguments. These were proclaimed 'weak, childish, and unphilosophical', inasmuch as they were founded upon the supposition, whose falsity Ramsay undertook later to prove both by scripture and reason, 'that moral and physical evil will be eternal and indestructible; and that what is indestructible must be self-existent'.[27] In Book III, which concerns the properties and differences of finite beings, Ramsay went some way towards this objective by endeavouring to establish the essential moral freedom of human creatures made in the divine image. Again a corollary was used in order to make the point that 'freedom is not an arbitrary gift of God as Bayle says, but a necessary, inseparable adjunct of our intelligent, reasonable natures'.[28] Such attacks on his treatment of the problem of evil and cognate issues culminate in Book VI, the subject of which is the universe in its re-established perfection. Here Ramsay, who credited Bayle with raising every possible objection against Providence in the *Dictionnaire* and the *Réponse aux questions d'un provincial*, presented and refuted the main facets of the governing hypothesis that 'moral and physical evil are to be eternal, the damned uncontrovertible, and God for ever unappeasable'. Once more Ramsay's own countervailing standpoint was that of a universalist.[29]

Elsewhere in Part I of the *Philosophical Principles* Ramsay thrice refers to Bayle in relation to other philosophers, among them Leibniz. The Chevalier makes the comment, which confirms his acquaintance with the *Théodicée*, that all Leibniz's answers to Bayle's objections 'turn upon this one idea, that the evils which happen are suffered, allowed, or permitted to procure the greatest of all goods'[30] (Book VI). Earlier, in Book III, Ramsay cites Bayle as an effective critic of the Occasionalism of Malebranche, another erstwhile guide with whom he was now at variance.[31] By contrast, in an appendix directed against the first book of Spinoza's *Ethics*, he not only disregarded Bayle's critique of Spinozism, which he maintained the latter had not understood, but amplified this judgement into a restatement of his declaration that Bayle was a superficial and inveterately sceptical thinker.[32]

Much more interesting than this carping denunciation of Bayle is the one reference to him contained in Part II of the *Philosophical Principles*, where, as in *Les Voyages de Cyrus*, Ramsay made the comparative study of religion an instrument of apologetics in an endeavour to show 'that Christianity is as old as the creation'.[33] Since this meant acknowledging an element of genuine inspiration in the sacred writings of pagan antiquity, he perforce attacked those of contrary persuasion, whom he classed as 'incredulous critics such as Bayle' and 'grammatical critics such as Scaliger and Casaubon'. For Ramsay, assured as he was that all other religions were fundamentally consonant with his own faith, it was the very clarity with which Christian doctrines had been prefigured in such sources as the Hermetic Egyptian books and the Chaldean, Persian, and Orphic oracles that had induced both groups of critics to pronounce them counterfeit, albeit for partly differing reasons: 'the first from a perverse opposition to, the last from a superstitious respect for the holy scriptures, and both from a profound ignorance of the great principles of the divine philosophy'.[34]

It is this concern for the 'divine philosophy', which was the enduring mainspring of Ramsay's life and literary career as an expatriate, that is likewise the essential clue to his attitude to Bayle, the drastic shift in which it cogently explains. In 1710, when Ramsay arrived on the Continent to intensify his quest for religious truth, Bayle had been opposed most vehemently by the very type of Calvinist against whom Ramsay was so strongly reacting. In addition, Bayle had similarly emigrated for religious reasons after having for a time been a convert to Roman Catholicism, a step Ramsay himself was shortly to take. There was consequently much in Bayle's reputation and career to send Ramsay enquiringly to his works, especially the noted *Dictionnaire*, which could now be consulted in either French or English and whose multifarious contents were such as to yield some philosophical insight which went well with 'inward religion'. Presumably one of the lost Ramsay manuscripts, the title of which was the sobriquet he had admiringly given to Bayle,[35] stemmed from this early phase of acknowledged indebtedness to Bayle the philosopher.

As the early decades of the eighteenth century progressed, however, Ramsay's estimate of Bayle was bound to change. For whereas the one felt impelled to become an apologist, the other became increasingly notorious as an archetypal free-thinker whose writings, editions of which were accumulating in post-Regency France, seemed repositories of irreligion and scepticism. It is no wonder that, in these altered circumstances, Ramsay should have critically reassessed Bayle's contribution to the pursuit of truth. Inevitably, too, he was bound to conclude that Bayle's endowments had been particularly ill spent in expounding those Manichean and Pyrrhonian arguments which had so contributed to what he obviously felt to be the growing need for the defence of natural and revealed religion enshrined in *Les Voyages de Cyrus* and the *Philosophical Principles*.

Yet if Bayle's ascertainable influence upon Ramsay concerns the content rather than the literary form of the latter's works, one curious further link between the two should not go unrecorded. In refuting the Origenism of Jean Le Clerc's *Parrhasiana* in remark E of the article Origène in the second (1702) edition of the *Dictionnaire*, Bayle alludes to 'un héros de roman formé pour être un modèle de la perfection royale, un prince, dis-je, tiré d'après les idées encore plus exactement que le Cyrus de Xenophon . . .' Exactly a quarter of a century later, Ramsay's *Voyages de Cyrus* not merely realized such a project but, by a curious contrast, did so in the service of Origenistic universalism. *Post hoc ergo propter hoc?* It would be rash to affirm the connection, especially since Fénelon's *Télémaque* is evidently the major inspiration of Ramsay's work; but there remains this intriguing possibility none the less.

A. W. FAIRBAIRN

REFERENCES

1 On Ramsay see A. Cherel, *Fénelon au XVIIIᵉ siècle en France*, Paris, 1917, the study of Ramsay which occupies pp. 31–151 being reproduced in almost identical form as *Un Aventurier religieux au XVIIIᵉ siècle*, *André-Michel Ramsay*, Paris, 1926. Also G. D. Henderson, *Chevalier Ramsay*, London, 1952.

2 *Journal encyclopédique*, 15 May 1771, t.4, pt 1, pp. 126–131. The conclusion of this letter contains an apparent reference to the recent appearance of C.-F. Houtteville's *La Religion chrétienne prouvée par les faits*, Paris, 1722, which was on sale early that year. Cf. Mathieu Marais, *Journal et Mémoires*, ed. Lescure, Paris, 1863–1868, t.3, pp. 505–507 (entry of 16 Feb., 1722); *Journal de Verdun*, March, 1722, pp. 163–166; *Journal des Savants*, April, 1722, pp. 363–373. Ramsay would seem to have written to la Motte about this time.

3   1st ed., Rotterdam, 1697, but cited in the 1720 Rotterdam ed.
4   1720 *D.H.C.*, t.4, p. 2913b. Cf. Bayle to Coste, 8 April 1704: 'Au reste, on ne saurait trouver dans son esprit, si l'on tâche de ne se pas faire illusion, l'idée d'une étendue qui ne soit point tout à fait semblable à l'étendue de la matière.' *Oeuvres diverses*, The Hague, 1725–1731, t.4, p. 841.
5   *Fénelon au XVIIIᵉ siècle en France*, p. 99.
6   1st ed., The Hague, 1719. Page refs. to the 3rd ed., 'Londres', 1722.
7   Ibid., pp. 37, 172–173. Cf. *O.D.*, t.2, p. 594.
8   Ibid., p. 175. Cf. *O.D.*, t.2, p. 602.
9   Paris, 1727. Page refs. to the Amsterdam ed. of 1728, 2 tomes.
10   Cf. art. Manichéens, rem. C; art. Zoroastre, rem. E.
11   Ed. cit., t.2, B, pp. 8–9.
12   Ibid., t.2, p. 20. Cf. *D.H.C.*, t.3, p. 1899.
13   Ibid., t.2, B, p. 82.
14   *Bibliothèque universelle des romans*, Dec., 1775, pp. 89–101.
15   Henderson, op. cit., p. 238.
16   *B.U.R.*, Dec., 1775, pp. 102–107.
17   Op. cit., t.3, pp. 505–507.
18   B.N., f. fr. 25541, ff. 178vo–179.
19   Op. cit., t.3, p. 509.
20   B.N., f. fr. 25541, f. 180vo.
21   B.N., f. fr. 25542, f. 259.
22   Pp. 694–720.
23   Ibid., p. 708. Cf. *B.U.R.*, Dec., 1775, p. 104. On the Origenism of More, see S. Hutin, *Henry More. Essai sur les doctrines théosophiques chez les Platoniciens de Cambridge*, Hildesheim, 1966, pp. 176–178.
24   Ibid., t.1, p. 21.
25   Ed. cit., t.2, p. 22, n.(b).
26   Ibid., t.1, p. 27.
27   Ibid., t.1, p. 50.
28   Ibid., t.1, p. 221. Cf. art. Rorarius, rem. F: 'Il est donc visible que la liberté d'indifférence n'est point un attribut essentiel de la créature, mais une concession, ou une faveur accidentelle dont le Créateur la gratifie.' Cf. also *R. aux Q.*, chaps. 138 foll., *O.D.*, t.3, pt 2, pp. 780 foll.
29   Ibid., t.1, pp. 478–480.
30   Ibid., t.1, p. 483.
31   Ibid., t.1, p. 267. Cf. art. Pauliciens, rem. F.
32   Ibid., t.1, p. 540.
33   Ibid., t.2, p. iii. Cf. Henderson, op. cit., p. 218.
34   Ibid., t.2, p. 59.
35   Henderson, op. cit., p. 243. Appendix II. Catalogue of manuscripts brought by Mr Foulis from France. Received by Francis Kennedy from Dr John Stevenson, 21 April 1744. Item 7: Démocrite français, 1 layer of 5 sheets.

FRENCH INFLUENCES ON BACH

In *L'art de toucher le clavecin*[1] Couperin wrote:

As the sounds of the harpsichord are isolated one from the other and as the power of each sound cannot be increased or diminished, it has hitherto appeared almost impossible for a player to bring expression to this instrument. But I shall try to show how, by research and with the aid of the little feeling that Heaven has given me, I have acquired the fortune to appeal to people of taste.

In these words Couperin saw clearly the great shortcomings of the harpsichord: tone could not be sustained nor could it be graded. If a greater or a smaller volume of tone was required it could only be obtained by writing for more or less parts—at least on the small instruments that Couperin used—and the harpsichord-player was felt to be at a disadvantage compared to the lutanist who 'could strike the strings of his instrument as forcefully or as lightly as he wished, could make them speak in fact, and could even by means of sound express tenderness and anger in varying degrees.'[2]

The harpsichord could easily be dull. How otherwise was it that 'Chambonnières sommeille dès que la première reprise est accomplie'? Or that, in the words of a contemporary, 'one dozed off to an allemande and awakened to a gigue.'[3] The problem that Couperin set himself was in some way to relieve the monotonous *tin-tin du clavecin* by artistic devices inherent in the harpsichord; and his means of appealing to 'people of taste' was by a carefully worked-out system of embellishments—trills, mordants, grace notes and turns—known as *manières*.

It has often been said that Bach's ornaments derive from the French clavecinists and in particular from the harpsichord music of Couperin, though he used them for different musical purposes. In French harpsichord music, the importance of the ornaments in regard to the musical skeleton, was that of pirouettes in a certain style of dancing or of curlicues in Baroque architecture. Some of them, it is true, were used to give accent or, such as the *tremblement*, to create the illusion of sustained tone by the repetition of two adjacent notes in rapid succession. But in the main they are an added grace of this music whereas in Bach they become fused with other elements of melodic design and form an imperceptible part of it. Thus it was that he extended and transformed a number of them.

First as to Bach's actual acquaintance with French music. As Bach never travelled out of Germany it may at first seem that he was less susceptible to foreign influences than Handel. Yet when Bach was over fifty Johann Adolph Scheibe wrote: 'German music has taken the greater part of its substance from abroad';[4] and four years after his death Marpurg remarked: 'In music the Germans have no taste of their own. Our Handel and Telemann resemble the French, and Hasse and Graun, the Italians.'[5] In Bach's youth, Germany was overrun with foreign musicians and there was no need to go abroad to study them. He first became acquainted with the methods of French composers at Celle although in the course of his life these methods filtered through to Germany from a number of sources. 'The things expressed by the French stenographic characters,' said Mr. Edward Dannreuther,[6]

> probably reached Bach from all parts of Europe—from the English virginal players and composers of the Parthenia through Sweelinck of Amsterdam and some of his many disciples, Buxtehude of Lübeck, Bruhns of Husum, Scheidt of Halle and Reinken of Hamburg—from Frescobaldi in Rome through his pupils Froberger and Franz Tunder,[7] who became organist at Lübeck —through the South German organist and cembalist Georg Muffat, who spent six years in Paris in Lully's time—from Pachelbel, organist at Nürnberg—from friends and colleagues whom Bach heard and admired in his youth, such as Georg Böhm, organist at Lüneburg, and Johann Gottfried Walther, organist at Weimar—from the older members of his own family— and even from Faustina Hasse and the vocalists of the Italian Opera at Dresden.

Bach's vists to Celle were around the year 1700. He had left Ohrdruf, where his brother was church organist, and had entered the Michaelisschule at Lüneburg. Here, when he was just fifteen, he first took certain musicians as his models: Böhm for composition, the veteran Reinken at Hamburg for the organ, and at Celle, some eighty kilometres from Lüneburg, the French musicians of the court of Georg Wilhelm, Duke of Braunschweig-Lüneburg, for clavier playing. This at least is what has been surmised.[8] The Duke was fond of living in Italy and France, and records show that his musicians were nearly all Frenchmen.[9]

It is not known what Bach did at Celle, whether he had some engagement to play in the orchestra or whether he merely came to listen. Pirro[10] remarks that one Charles Gaudon, the court organist, might have initiated Bach in French keyboard practices; that at the court concerts he might have heard the overtures of Lully; or that the French refugees at Celle and at Lüneburg (the Duke's wife, Eléonore Desmier d'Olbreuze, was herself a Huguenot) had in their possession manuscripts of French music which Bach would have known. What one can point to with more certainty are copies of Nicholas de Grigny's *Livre d'Orgue* and of two Suites of Dieupart, to which was appended a table of ornaments, made by Bach at this time.[11] Also it was probably due to his acquaintance with French compositions at Celle that a great number of them found their way into his pupils' manuscript collections.[12]

At Lüneburg Bach must have been considerably impressed with Böhm, the organist of the Johanniskirche, for twenty years later he includes a 'Menuet fait par Mons. Böhm' in Anna Magdalena's *Notenbuch*—an unobtrusive little composition that might have come out of an opera by Lully. That Bach attached importance to the proper playing of ornaments in the French manner is shown by the great number of highly decorated pieces in the two *Notenbücher of* Anna Magdalena (1722 and 1725) and in the *Clavier-Büchlein für Wilhelm Friedemann* (1720) which he intended his wife and son to practise. The Rondeau on page 27 of the Bachgesellschaft edition of Anna Magdelena's *Notenbuch* is actually a composition of

Couperin, 'Les Bergeries'. Judging from the *Explication unter-schiedlicher Zeichen* in Wilhelm Friedemann's *Clavier-Büchlein*, Bach must have been well acquainted with Couperin's harpsichord music. The resemblance between Bach's and Couperin's *manières* is striking. The *trillo* (Ex. 1a) is the *tremblement détaché* (Ex. 1b) given in the *Explication des agréments et des signes* in Couperin's *Pièces de Clavecin*; the *mordant* (Ex. 1c) is the *pincé simple* (Ex. 1d); the *cadence* (Ex. 1e) is the *double* (Ex. 1f); the *accent und mordant* (Ex. 1g), the *port de voix simple* (Ex. 1h); and the *accent steigend* (Ex. 1i) the *port de voix coulée* (Ex. 1j).

Ex 1

Bach's list is completed by a number of combined ornaments but no mention is made of the so-called *willkürliche Manieren*.[13] These consisted of passing notes, suspensions and anticipations, sometimes left to the discretion of the performer but generally written out in detail. Such ornaments may be found in the *Double* that follows the *Sarabande* of the third English Suite—'Les Agréments de la même Sarabande'—in which Bach follows Couperin's practice of giving an alternative version of his dances.[14] But here the style of ornamentation is not French but Italian. Wanda Landowska[15] observes this ornate method in the *andante* of the Italian Concerto. It was such works, apparently, that caused J. A. Scheibe to write of Bach:

> This great man would be the wonder of all nations if he had more grace and if he did not make his pieces sound unnatural by the use of high-flown, complicated devices, thus obscuring the real beauty of his music by too grandiose a conception of art. His compositions are extremely difficult to perform for his standard is the dexterity of his own fingers and he expects singers and instrumentalists to obtain the same effects as he does himself at the keyboard. This is impossible. All the ornaments and grace notes *Alle Manieren, alle kleine Auszierungen,* all that one expects in accomplished playing, he writes out in full, which not only deprives his pieces of their harmonic beauty but makes the melody unintelligible. In a word, he is in music what von Lohenstein was once in poetry. Their bombastic style has led them both to fall from the natural to the artificial and from the sublime to the obscure. One admires their toil and extraordinary pains, but as their efforts are contrary to reason they are in vain.

The use of French ornaments in Bach is to be found in the great number of works like the *allemande* of the second French suite.

The figures in bars one and two (first beats) are really a form of the *tierce coulée* described by Couperin (Ex. 3a) or of the *chute sur deux*

notes (Ex. 3b) mentioned in the preface to Henry d'Anglebert's
Pièces de Clavecin.[16]

Ex 3

In the second beat of the second bar Couperin's *pincé* is simply written
out in full and in the third beat of the same bar is an inversion of
Couperin's *double*. (See Exs. 1d and 1f). At the double bar the
ornaments become:

Ex 4

and it is interesting to note how Bach's use of passing notes, deriving
in part from the *tierce coulée* is extended to the diminished fifth:

Ex 5

From here it is only a step to the use of an ornamental figure as
a fugue subject. The subject of Fugue 5 of the 'Forty-eight'
(Ex. 6a) is in origin the *tremblement et pincé* noted in d'Anglebert's
Pièces de Clavecin (Ex. 6b).

The dotted crotchet progression which completes the subject is reminiscent too of French technique. 'When the French consider placing dots after notes they regard them as salt in cooking.'[17] Pirro[18] observes that it was the practice of French composers to introduce dots at discretion. Couperin's statement in *L'Art de toucher le clavecin* seems to confirm this: 'Nous pointons plusieurs croches de suite par degrés conjoints; et cependant nous les marquons égales'. And it was a procedure used by Bach in a passage in Contrapunctus VI, *in stile francese*, of the *Kunst der Fuge*; in the Overture and Partita in B minor, *nach französischer Art*; and in number XVI of the Goldberg variations. The last is in the form of a French *ouverture*[19] and a comparison of this with the overture to 'Les Saisons' by Lully is instructive of how much Bach was indebted to the French for rhythmic design.

The overture was of course not the only form in which Bach adhered to French models. Wanda Landowska gives a complete list of the well-known dance forms which Bach used.[20] In vocal music he was influenced by the *air à deux*[21] which, Mattheson said, 'may be written in the Italian or the French manner. The French *airs à deux* require a note-against-note counterpoint (*lieben den gleichen Contrapunct*) and as the two voices sing the same words at the same time there is little or no concerted writing.'[22] An example of this is the 'Duo de Zéphire et Flore' from Lully's 'Les Saisons':

and in Bach the great *Et misericordia* from the Magnificat in D.

Finally there is the question of fingering. Bach and Couperin were the first in their respective countries to advocate the use of the thumb both as a pivot and for greater stretch. It has been suggested that Bach was acquainted with Couperin's method of fingering and that this was the subject of some correspondence between them.[23] It is doubtful that he was acquainted with it from *L'Art de toucher le clavecin*. If he were, one would expect this work to be mentioned in

Ph. Em. Bach's *Versuch*. Philip Emmanuel, however, regrets, in his work, not having the advantage of a precursor. Nor, since this correspondence is irrecoverably lost, can any discussion arise on Monsieur A. Gastoué's suggestion of attributing it to a parallel which he draws between certain religious compositions of Couperin and the St. Matthew Passion.[24] What Athanasius Kircher,[25] thirty-five years before Bach was born, and Mattheson,[26] when he was over fifty, noted and recommended in French music was the *stylus hyporchematicus*.[27] The art in which the French excelled was dancing; the music—solo-songs with lute accompaniment in the seventeenth century, harpsichord pieces in the eighteenth—was merely accessory. In Germany these dance tunes became themselves artistic entities no longer requiring a dance to excuse them; and so it was that ornamentation grew into design and the frills that covered pegs of notes became an essential part of figuration. In this connection it is not irrelevant to note that figures constantly appearing in the works of nineteenth-century composers such as those in the Beethoven sonata in B flat, op. 22 (Ex. 11), and in the prelude to 'Götterdämmerung' (Ex. 12)

have their origin in the incorporation of French *manières* in the language of Bach.

EDWARD LOCKSPEISER

Reprinted, in a revised form, from *Music and Letters*, October, 1935, founded and edited by the writer and musician A. H. Strangways.

REFERENCES

1 Paris, 1717.
2 See André Pirro, *Les Clavecinistes*, Paris, 1924, p. 91.
3 Ibid., p. 60.
4 *Der Critische Musikus*, Leipzig, 2nd ed. 1745.
5 *Historisch-Kritische Beyträge zur Aufnahme der Musik*. See André Pirro, *L'Esthétique de Jean Sébastien Bach*, Paris, 1907, p. 436.
6 *Musical Ornamentation*, London, 1893, p. ix.
7 Tunder is a mistake. He died eighteen years before Bach was born and was succeeded at Lübeck by Buxtehude.
8 See A. Pirro, *Bach*, p. 422.
9 See C. S. Terry, *Bach : a biography*, London, 1933, p. 50.
10 See A. Pirro, *Bach*, pp. 422 and 424.
11 Dannreuther, op. cit., p. 138, says: 'There can be no doubt that Bach took many a hint from Dieupart. There is an unmistakable flavour of Bach in Dieupart's Allemandes, Courantes and Gigues and the slow portions of Dieupart's Ouvertures shadow forth similar movements of Bach's—thus the Ouverture to the Partita in B minor, for a harpsichord with two keyboards, the companion piece to the Italian concerto, Clavierübung II, is simply Dieupart transfigured and glorified.'
12 Pirro, *Bach*, p. 431, states that in the notebook of Krebs, a pupil of Bach, are suites by Gaspard le Roux and Dieupart. A gigue of the latter bears a striking resemblance to the prelude of Bach's first English suite.
13 See C. P. E. Bach, *Versuch über die wahre Art das Clavier zu spielen*. Berlin, 1753.
14 See *Pièces de Clavecin*, first book—*Courante avec le dessus plus orné sans changer la basse*.
15 *Musique Ancienne*, Paris, 1909.
16 Paris, 1689.
17 J. Mattheson, *Kern Melodischer Wissenchaft*, Hamburg, 1737, p. 64.
18 *L'Esthétique de J. S. Bach*, p. 439.
19 Dannreuther, op. cit., p. 200, says that the French ouverture 'generally opens with a stately movement in square time built upon simple progressions in the bass. Divisions were written out in plain notes but the players were at liberty to introduce further ornaments and they did so.'
20 *Bach–Jahrbuch*, 1910, p. 43. They are: the courante, sarabande, gavotte, musette, passepied, bourrée, menuet, air, allemande, anglaise, loure, gigue, rondeau and polonaise.
21 See Pirro, *Bach*, p. 317.
22 Op cit., p. 99.
23 See C. Bouvet, *Les Couperin, une dynastie de musiciens français*, Paris, 1919. 'The mother of Alexandre Taskin, a singer at the Opéra comique, states that there had been some correspondence between J. S. Bach and Couperin, a distant relative of hers, in which Bach declares his indebtedness to Couperin; she also says that the letter or letters in question were used to cover jam pots with'. This information was given to Monsieur Bouvet by Madame Arlette Taskin.
24 *François Couperin, musicien religieux dramatique, et J. S. Bach*, by A. Gastoué. *La Revue Musicale*, Paris, December, 1932.
25 *Musurgia Universalis*, Rome, 1650.
26 Op. cit., p. 22. 'Die hohe Tanz-Kunst auf Schaubühnen hat, in den dazu geschickten Melodien und Sätzen, ihren ganz eigenen Styl,

nehmlich den hyporchematischen, der die Chaconnen, Passacaglien, Entreen und andre grosse Tänze liefert, welche sehr offt nicht nur gespielet, sondern auch mit vielen angenehmen Abwechslungen gesungen werden. In Erkänntniss dieser Schreib-Art thun wenig ausgesuchte Französische Sachen mehr Dienste als alle Welsche: denn Frankreich ist und bleibet die rechte Tanz-Schule.'

27 *Hyporchematicus*, ' a dance with singing.'

THE *PHILOSOPHES* AND THE IDEA OF PROGRESS

This modest contribution to the discussion of a vast subject was inspired partly by meditation on the paper read by Norman Suckling at the second international congress on the Enlightenment, held at St. Andrews in 1967,[1] and partly by renewed contact with Condorcet's *Esquisse d'un tableau historique des progrès de l'esprit humain.* In the last twenty years the pioneer work of J. B. Bury on the idea of progress, published in 1920, has been supplemented by other general books such as C. Frankel's *The Faith of Reason : the Idea of Progress in the French Enlightenment* (New York, 1948), M. Ginsberg's *The Idea of Progress : a Revaluation* (London, 1953) and R. V. Sampson's *Progress in the Age of Reason* (London, 1956). More recently two books with oddly contrasting titles have appeared which concentrate on the eighteenth century, though without limiting themselves to a discussion of the idea of progress in that period : H. Vyverberg's *Historical Pessimism in the French Enlightenment* (Harvard, 1958) and *Eighteenth-Century Optimism* by my Durham colleague, Charles Vereker (Liverpool, 1967).

If an undergraduate studying Condorcet could be induced to work his way through these varied publications, he would form a somewhat confused picture of the relationship between the ideas on progress set down at the height of the Terror by this disciple of the *philosophes*, and the ideas and hopes which they themselves entertained about the future of humanity. That there was a gulf between his outlook and that of such older contemporaries as Voltaire, D'Alembert, Diderot, Helvétius or D'Holbach was made perfectly clear by Condorcet himself when in the *IXe époque* he came to discuss the development of the notion of the indefinite perfectibility of the human race. It is not to them that he attributes the holding of any such idea :

Enfin, on vit se développer une doctrine nouvelle, qui devait

C*

porter le dernier coup à l'édifice déjà chancelant des préjugés: c'est celle de la perfectibilité indéfinie de l'espèce humaine, doctrine dont Turgot, Price et Priestley ont été les premiers et les plus illustres apôtres.[2]

No doubt Condorcet would have been delighted to have been able to invoke the authority of the older generation of *philosophes*, starting with Voltaire himself, in support of his theory. Instead he had to content himself with quoting Turgot, flanked by two English writers whose contribution to the new theory was pretty negligible.[3]

It is inevitable, since they all cover a span of several centuries, that general works on the idea of progress such as those of Bury, Frankel, Ginsberg and Sampson should only dwell briefly on the writings of the *philosophes* and their contribution to the development of this concept. They can do little more than hint at the complexity of the attitudes of individual thinkers like Voltaire or Diderot. Though Vyverberg's work, being devoted to the French Enlightenment, does come much closer to the thought of these men, his elucidation of their outlook is naturally restricted by his stress on one aspect of their thought—their historical pessimism—and, less justifiably, by the extraordinarily wide area over which he spreads his net. It takes in the seventeenth century as well as the eighteenth. In the former period he deals with many writers (Bossuet, Boileau and Fénelon, for instance) whose connection with the Enlightenment is, to put it mildly, extremely tenuous; and for the latter period, far from concentrating on the group of writers who were the standard-bearers of the Enlightenment, he meanders all over eighteenth-century French thought. Vereker's work, which covers English as well as French thought, inevitably concentrates on the other side of the medal and tends to play down the pessimistic side of the thought of the French Enlightenment. Putting together the comments of these various works on the attitude of the *philosophes* to the idea of progress scarcely produces a clear picture.

That, in their writings in the 1750's and 1760's, the *philosophes* showed their pride in the progress achieved by man since the

Renaissance is perfectly clear. In the second part of the *Discours préliminaire* which he produced for the *Encyclopédie*, D'Alembert composed a hymn to the progress achieved by man since 'la renaissance des lettres'. Nowhere is the pride of this group in the accomplishments of men in the last two or three centuries more eloquently conveyed than in the opening lines of Rousseau's *Discours sur les sciences et les arts*, published in the previous year:

> C'est un grand et beau spectacle de voir l'homme sortir en quelque manière du néant par ses propres efforts; dissiper, par les lumières de sa raison, les ténèbres dans lesquelles la nature l'avait enveloppé; s'élever au-dessus de soi-même; s'élancer par l'esprit jusque dans les régions célestes; parcourir à pas de géant, ainsi que le soleil, la vaste étendue de l'univers; et, ce qui est encore plus grand et plus difficile, rentrer en soi pour y étudier l'homme et connaître sa nature, ses devoirs et sa fin. Toutes ces merveilles se sont renouvelées depuis peu de générations.

Yet it is notorious that one seeks in vain in the *Encyclopédie* itself for any consistent theory of progress. All one finds under this headword in one of the last ten volumes published in 1765 is a brief, unsigned grammatical article (it could well have been by Diderot himself):

> PROGRES, s.m. (*Gramm.*) mouvement en avant, le *progrès* du soleil dans l'écliptique; le *progrès* du feu; le *progrès* de cette racine. Il se prend aussi au figuré, et l'on dit *faire des progrès* rapides dans un art, dans une science.

The fact is that, whatever their pride in the intellectual and other achievements of man, neither of the two editors held the starry-eyed vision of his future progress which has often been attributed to the *philosophes* in general. For all his satisfaction with advances made by man since the Renaissance, D'Alembert concludes this section of the *Discours préliminaire* with some very gloomy remarks on the subject of human history. Far from being held enthralled by a vision of man marching 'on and on and on, and up and up and up', he clearly states his belief in an alternation of light and darkness in the history of man, in which for most of the time darkness wins:

> ... Tout a des révolutions réglées, et l'obscurité se terminera par un nouveau siècle de lumière. Nous serons plus frappés du grand jour après avoir été quelque temps dans les ténèbres. Elles seront comme une espèce d'anarchie très funeste par elle-même, mais quelquefois utile par ses suites. Gardons-nous pourtant de souhaiter une révolution si redoutable; la barbarie dure des siècles, il semble que ce soit notre élément; la raison et le bon goût ne font que passer.[4]

In other words, in the intellectual as in the aesthetic sphere, the triumph of light over darkness can only be shortlived.

Similar views emerge from Diderot's own editorial contribution on the aims of an encyclopedia in the article *ENCYCLOPÉDIE which appeared in 1755 in the fifth volume. No doubt the whole enterprise had been conceived as an attempt to enlighten men and to diffuse among a wider public the results of the progress so far achieved in thought, science and technology. The aim of an encyclopedia, Diderot tells us at the beginning of the article, is to provide in one massive work a sum of human knowledge and to transmit it to future generations in order that 'nos neveux, devenant plus instruits, deviennent en même temps plus vertueux et plus heureux, et que nous ne mourions pas sans avoir bien mérité du genre humain'.[5] Implicit in the whole undertaking was a belief in the future progress —moral as well as intellectual—of the human race. Yet nowhere does Diderot express clearly and unambiguously a belief in such progress.

Indeed at moments he took an extremely gloomy view of the possibility of enlightening even his contemporaries. In a letter to Voltaire, written it is true in 1758 when the attacks of the enemies of the *Encyclopédie* had brought the whole enterprise to a standstill, he is seen plunged in pessimism about human nature:

> *Etre utile aux hommes?* Est-il bien sûr qu'on fasse autre chose que les amuser, et qu'il y ait grande différence entre le philosophe et le joueur de flûte? Ils écoutent l'un et l'autre avec plaisir ou dédain, et demeurent ce qu'ils sont.[6]

While in typical Diderot fashion he goes on to admit to Voltaire that this is a somewhat exaggerated view of the situation, this is by no means the only occasion on which he expresses such pessimistic views. In the preface which he composed for the last ten volumes of the *Encyclopédie* his pleasure at having brought the text of the work to completion is far from unalloyed. We find there in the very first paragraph these gloomy reflexions:

Le monde a beau vieillir, il ne change pas; il se peut que l'individu se perfectionne, mais la masse de l'espèce ne devient ni meilleure ni pire; la somme des passions malfaisantes reste la même, et les ennemis de toute chose bonne et utile sont sans nombre comme autrefois.[7]

Once again, this observation must not be taken out of its context; it reflects the editor's anger at the obstacles which powerful enemies had placed in the way of the *Encyclopédie*.

Yet one need go no further than the article *ENCYCLOPÉDIE in order to discover that, like D'Alembert, Diderot saw only very limited possibilities of progress, even in the intellectual sphere:

Cependant les connaissances ne deviennent et ne peuvent devenir communes que jusqu'à un certain point. On ignore, à la vérité, quelle est cette limite. On ne sait jusqu'où tel homme peut aller. On sait bien moins encore jusqu'où l'espèce humaine irait, ce dont elle serait capable, si elle n'était point arrêtée dans ses progrès. Mais les révolutions sont nécessaires; il y en a toujours eu, et il y en aura toujours; le plus grand intervalle d'une révolution à une autre est donné. Cette seule cause borne l'étendue de nos travaux.[8]

What sort of cataclysm Diderot had in mind as limiting the intellectual progress of mankind is never made exactly clear, though some light is thrown on the question by another passage in the same article, one which aroused hilarity among contemporary critics of the work:

Le moment le plus glorieux pour un ouvrage de cette nature, ce serait celui qui succéderait immédiatement à quelque grande révolution qui aurait suspendu les progrès des sciences, interrompu les travaux des arts, et replongé dans les ténèbres une portion de notre hémisphère. Quelle reconnaissance la génération qui viendrait après ces temps de trouble ne porterait-elle pas aux hommes qui les auraient redoutés de loin, et qui en auraient prévenu le ravage, en mettant à l'abri les connaissances des siècles passés![9]

Diderot sees then decided limits to the intellectual progress of both the species and the individual:

Il y a dans les sciences un point au delà duquel il ne leur est presque pas accordé de passer. Lorsque ce point est atteint, les monuments qui restent de ce progrès sont à jamais l'étonnement de l'espèce entière. Mais si l'espèce est bornée dans ses efforts, combien l'individu ne l'est-il pas dans les siens?[10]

For Diderot then, as for D'Alembert, there can be no question of believing in the indefinite perfectibility of the human species.

It is astonishing to find that Naigeon, Diderot's first biographer, writing after the publication of Condorcet's *Esquisse*, tries to make out that this passage from *ENCYCLOPÉDIE exhibits the same faith in human perfectibility:

Il avance sur le perfectionnement indéfini de l'esprit humain, une opinion que Condorcet a portée depuis à ce degré de probabilité qui équivaut à la certitude; c'est que si on ignore jusqu'où tel homme peut aller, on sait bien moins encore jusqu'où l'espèce humaine irait, ce dont elle serait capable, si elle n'était point arrêtée dans ses progrès.

The next sentence begins with a 'Mais' and, as we shall see, it is a large 'But':

Mais Diderot me paraît attribuer trop d'influence aux révolutions nécessaires qui s'opposent à ces progrès; et, de ce qu'il y aura des ouvrages qui resteront toujours au-dessus de la portée commune des hommes, il ne s'ensuit point, ce me semble, que l'espèce soit bornée dans ses efforts, et l'individu dans les siens.[11]

Translated into plain English, this simply means that in practice, the ideas of Diderot and Condorcet are miles apart. One searches in vain in Diderot's writings for a coherent theory of progress.

What of Voltaire's ideas in the 1750's and 1760's? This is the period not only of *Candide*, but of his great historical works—*Le Siècle de Louis XIV* (1751) and his universal history, *L'Essai sur les mœurs et l'esprit des nations* (1756). Neither of these could be said to make the past history of mankind serve as a foundation for a belief in the indefinite perfectibility of the human race. In the introduction to *Le Siècle de Louis XIV* Voltaire declares:

... Quiconque pense, et, ce qui est encore plus rare, quiconque a du goût, ne compte que quatre siècles dans l'histoire du monde. Ces quatre âges heureux sont ceux où les arts ont été perfectionnés, et qui, servant d'époque à la grandeur de l'esprit humain, sont l'exemple de la postérité.[12]

These four ages—those of Philip and Alexander, Caesar and Augustus, the Renaissance, and Louis XIV—represent, taken altogether, only a small part of recorded history. 'Tous les siècles', Voltaire adds, 'se ressemblent par la méchanceté des hommes; mais je ne connais que ces quatre âges distingués par les grands talents.'[13]

L'Essai sur les mœurs is even further from giving one the impression that Voltaire sought to base on the past history of man a prediction of his future development towards increasing enlightenment and happiness. That civilization had made progress since the barbarian invasions was clear, but to Voltaire the historian man's past gave one no grounds for believing in a rosy future. At the end of his universal history he exclaims with disgust:

Il faut donc, encore une fois, avouer qu'en général toute cette histoire est un ramas de crimes, de folies et de malheurs, parmi lesquels nous avons vu quelques vertus, quelques temps heureux, comme on découvre des habitations répandues çà et là dans les déserts sauvages.[14]

On the whole question of the possibility of future progress Voltaire here remains discreetly silent.

There is, however, one passage from his historical writings which Bury[15] and others after him quote; this passage merits close examination from various points of view. It first appears in Vol. XVIII, published in 1763, of the *Collection complète des œuvres de*

M. de Voltaire; Vols. XI–XVIII of this edition contain *L'Essai sur les Mœurs*, followed by *Le Siècle de Louis XIV*, merged into a work with the general title of *L'Essai sur l'histoire générale et sur les mœurs et l'esprit des nations depuis Charlemagne jusqu'à nos jours*. The whole work is rounded off with a chapter entitled 'Conclusion et examen de ce tableau historique' in which we find the passage in question, hidden away in the second half of a paragraph.

> Enfin, il est à croire que la raison et l'industrie feront toujours de nouveaux progrès, que les arts utiles prendront des accroissements, que parmi les maux qui ont affligé les hommes, les préjugés, qui ne sont pas leur moindre fléau, disparaîtront peu à peu chez tous ceux qui sont à la tête des nations; et que la philosophie partout plus répandue consolera un peu la nature humaine des calamités qu'elle éprouvera dans tous les temps.[16]

The extremely cautious nature of these predictions makes it easy to see why Condorcet did not seek to enlist Voltaire among the holders of a belief in the indefinite perfectibility of man; the gulf between these few lines and the X^e *époque* of his *Esquisse* is enormous. What is more, according to Beuchot,[17] this whole chapter was suppressed in later editions of the historical writings produced during Voltaire's lifetime. There is no evidence that he attached any great importance to this oft-quoted passage.

The radicals among the *philosophes*—D'Holbach and Helvétius —are often credited with views a little closer to those of Condorcet. D'Holbach was undoubtedly one of the most tireless (and, it must be said, tedious) propagandists among the *philosophes*. Such intense activity in assailing the prejudices and errors which were at the root of man's ills, would seem to imply a faith in the future progress of the human race. Yet, despite some moments of cheerful hope, D'Holbach often expresses his doubts quite openly. The past history of man can scarcely encourage great faith in his future progress. The study of history, he declares, is only useful 'parce qu'elle nous fournit des preuves multipliées des effets redoutables qu'ont produits sur la terre les passions et les délires des hommes.'[18] Writing from the Baron's country house in 1760 to Sophie Volland,

Diderot gives us a vivid picture of the gloomy view of man's past and of human nature which D'Holbach derived from his study of history:

> Le baron se tue de lire l'histoire qui ne sert qu'à lui gâter l'esprit et à lui aigrir le cœur. Il n'en retient que les atrocités de l'homme et de la nature. Il y apprend à mépriser et à haïr de plus en plus ses semblables. Y rencontre-t-il quelques pages noires à faire trembler, il a une joie secrète de m'en régaler.[19]

It was unlikely that a very rosy view of the future of man would be derived from such an attitude to history. For D'Holbach, as for many of the *philosophes*, writing as they were some twenty or thirty years before the great upheaval of 1789, the best hope of progress seemed to lie in the emergence of an enlightened ruler, 'un roi philosophe', who, surrounded by enlightened ministers and counsellors, would carry through the reforms which they were demanding with increasing urgency. At moments D'Holbach appears optimistic about the possibility of such a miracle actually occurring; at others he is sunk in gloom. 'A peine en mille ans', he exlaims on one occasion, 'rencontre-t-on dans l'histoire un souverain qui ait le mérite, les talents, la vertu d'un homme ordinaire!'[20]

Of the two men Helvétius was perhaps the more optimistic about the future. In his posthumous work, *De l'Homme*, we find, for instance, the following passage:

> Toute sage législation qui lie l'intérêt particulier à l'intérêt public, et fonde la vertu sur l'avantage de chaque individu, est indestructible. Mais cette législation est-elle possible? Pourquoi non? L'horizon de nos idées s'étend de jour en jour; et si la législation, comme les autres sciences, participe aux progrès de l'esprit humain, pourquoi désespérer du bonheur futur de l'humanité? Pourquoi les nations, s'éclairant de siècle en siècle, ne parviendraient-elles pas un jour à toute la plénitude du bonheur dont elles sont susceptibles? Ce ne serait pas sans peine que je me détacherais de cet espoir.[21]

Yet even a passage like this, more or less isolated in a long work, is far removed from Condorcet's *X^e époque*.

The *philosophe* who is generally held to stand closest to Condorcet is the Chevalier de Chastellux whose *De la Félicité publique* appeared in 1772. Though he died in 1788, he was only nine years older than Condorcet and thus belongs, like him, to the younger group of *philosophes* who were born some two to three decades after men of the generation of Diderot and D'Alembert. Even though it is possible to see in him a precursor of Condorcet, it is a by no means easy task to extract from the five hundred pages of *De la Félicité publique* a coherent theory of progress.

The sub-title of the work, *Considérations sur le sort des hommes dans les différentes époques de l'histoire*, gives a clearer impression of its contents than the title proper. What we are in fact offered here is an examination of the lot of men over the whole range of history, from the time of the ancient Egyptians down to the author's own day. The main thesis of the work tends to disappear under a deluge of facts and theories and digressions. Eventually it seems to have occurred to the author himself that the work lacked a conclusion to draw together the threads of his argument. He therefore added to a revised edition[22] both a new preface and a final chapter entitled 'Vues ultérieures sur la félicité publique'. Here he obligingly summarizes under twelve points his main arguments. From our present point of view the most important of these are the last two:

11°. Que les malheurs de l'humanité doivent bien moins être imputés à l'insuffisance ou à l'abus de la raison, qu'à l'ignorance des siècles passés, dans lesquels se sont formés la plupart des habitudes et des principes qui nous gouvernent encore.

12°. Qu'il y a donc tout à espérer du progrès des lumières; qu'elles ont amélioré et qu'elles améliorent journellement le sort des hommes; enfin, que loin d'avoir à envier les siècles passés, nous devons nous regarder comme beaucoup plus heureux que les anciens, vérité qui a été l'objet de cet ouvrage.[23]

The whole weight of this work is thus placed on the author's account of the state of mankind in the various stages of its history. Not only is there really almost nothing to correspond to the picture of the golden future awaiting mankind which Condorcet sketches out in his

X^e *époque*, but the account given of the past and present state of man offers only the most occasional observations on what lies in store for him. It is in practice very difficult to find more than an odd passage, scattered here and there in the long account of man's past history, which actually refers to his future. One of the few interesting pieces which one can detach for the purpose of quotation is one which occurs at the beginning of the chapter on the influence of the Renaissance on the lot of mankind:

> Nous avons voulu examiner si les hommes avaient atteint jusqu'ici le degré de bonheur auquel ils peuvent prétendre dans l'état de la société; et non contents d'avoir prouvé qu'ils en étaient restés très éloignés, nous avons cru devoir entrer dans quelques détails sur les obstacles qui ont dû retarder leurs progrès. Nous avons interrogé l'histoire, et dans plusieurs milliers d'années que ses fastes nous ont offertes, nous n'avons que trop bien reconnu la proportion des causes avec les effets; nous ne sommes que trop bien convaincus que, non seulement les peuples n'avaient pas connu le vrai bonheur, mais encore qu'ils n'avaient jamais pris le chemin qui pouvait les y conduire. Notre surprise a diminué, mais notre affliction s'est augmentée, lorsque nous nous sommes assurés que les gouvernements les plus estimés, les législations les plus révérées, n'ont jamais tendu à cette unique fin de tout gouvernement, *le plus grand bonheur du plus grand nombre d'individus.*

So much for the past. What of the future?

> Mais en récompense à cette triste vue sur le passé, nous avons senti naître en nous-mêmes un espoir bien doux pour les siècles à venir, une opinion bien consolante sur le siècle présent. Nous avons moins admiré nos ancêtres; mais nous avons mieux aimé nos contemporains, et plus espéré de nos neveux. Il ne nous reste donc plus qu'à lever toutes les objections qui pourraient empêcher le lecteur de partager cette disposition. C'est pourquoi nous essayerons de lui prouver: 1°. qu'il existe maintenant un principe de perfectibilité, une cause d'amélioration; 2°. que ce principe et cette cause ont déjà agi d'une manière très sensible.[24]

The final view which one takes away from a reading of *De la Félicité publique* is that, while Chastellux devotes some five hundred pages to proving at considerable length that the lot of man is better in the eighteenth century than in any previous age, his faith in his future progress is nothing like as robust as that of Condorcet. He stands closer to Voltaire and the Encyclopaedists than to the author of the *Esquisse*.

It would be well to exaggerate neither the optimism nor the pessimism of the *philosophes*. The recent works of Vereker and Vyverberg seem strangely one-sided in their whole approach to these questions. The *philosophes'* outlook on the world could be described as fundamentally optimistic in the sense that they believed that, since the sufferings and misfortunes of humanity were due to ignorance and prejudice, these could be removed by the spread of enlightenment. Yet though they were proud of the progress achieved since the Renaissance in so many spheres and proud of living in what they called 'un siècle philosophe', they were clearly far from sharing Condorcet's vision of mankind moving steadily upwards towards ever greater perfection.

J. LOUGH

REFERENCES

1 'The Enlightenment and the Idea of Progress' (published in *Studies on Voltaire and the Eighteenth Century*, Vol. LVIII, pp. 1461–1480).
2 *Esquisse*, Ed. O. H. Prior, Paris, 1933, p. 166.
3 See J. Lough, 'Condorcet et Richard Price' (*Revue de littérature comparée*, 1950, pp. 87–93).
4 *Discours préliminaire de l'Encyclopédie*, Ed. F. Picavet, Paris, 1919, p. 124.
5 *Oeuvres complètes*, Ed. J. Assézat and M. Tourneux, Paris, 1875–1877, 20 vols., Vol. XIV, p. 415.
6 *Correspondance*, Ed. G. Roth, Paris, 1955– (in course of publication), Vol. II, p. 39.
7 *Oeuvres complètes*, Vol. XIII, p. 171.
8 *Oeuvres complètes*, Vol. XIV, p. 427.
9 *Oeuvres complètes*, Vol. XIV, p. 428.
10 *Oeuvres complètes*, Vol. XIV, p. 427.
11 *Mémoires historiques et philosophiques sur la vie et les ouvrages de D. Diderot*, Paris, 1821, p. 81.
12 *Le Siècle de Louis XIV*, Ed. E. Bourgeois, Paris, n.d., pp. 1–2.
13 *Le Siècle de Louis XIV*, p. 4.

14   *L'Essai sur les Moeurs*, Ed. R. Pomeau, Paris, 1963, 2 vols., Vol. II, p. 804.
15   *The Idea of Progress*, pp. 149–150.
16   P. 340.
17   See Voltaire, *Oeuvres complètes*, Ed. L. Moland, Paris, 1877–1885, 52 vols., Vol. XXIV, p. 473 n.
18   *La Morale universelle*, Amsterdam, 1776, 3 vols., Vol. III, p. 46.
19   *Correspondance*, Vol. III, p. 212.
20   *La Politique naturelle*, London, 1773, Discours IX, chap. xxiv.
21   Section X, Chap. iv.
22   Bouillon, 1776, 2 vols. (The Newcastle University Library has another edition of 1776, published in Amsterdam by M. M. Rey, but this simply reproduces the text of 1772.)
23   Vol. II, p. 322.
24   Vol. II, pp. 81–82.

A BIBLICAL 'CONTE PHILOSOPHIQUE':
VOLTAIRE'S *TAUREAU BLANC*

For many years I have known Norman Suckling, for three of them I had the privilege of working alongside him; may this modest tribute, whatever its defects, be at least a token of the affection and esteem in which I hold him.

'Le patriarche avait vidé son sac.' So begins René Pomeau's admirable edition of *Le Taureau blanc*.[1] Voltaire has reached old age; his life's work over, he is calm in mind, all passion spent. He knows that his creative talent is declining, that death is near, that he cannot even hope to see Paris again[2]—all bitter blows; yet he avoids this ultimate trap of sourness, of cynical and sterile old age. The correspondence goes on as before, little abated and as full of spirit as ever; while from his almost empty bag he produces one more minor masterpiece, *Le Taureau blanc*. Only M. Pomeau, of all Voltaire's critics, has ever paid this little story anything but a casual glance. Yet to my mind it is one of Voltaire's most ingenious *contes*, substituting for the wit of *Candide* and the satiric pathos of *L'Ingénu* a more indirect approach, where the irony is linked to fantasy and the dream-world of a Voltairean Old Testament.

But when was this story written? M. Pomeau, after a comprehensive survey of the problem, admits that it cannot be solved with any certainty, but inclines to place the first edition in 1771–1772, with a further revision in 1773. This argument he bases upon the textual analogies he discovers between *Le Taureau blanc* and other writings of the same period (pp. xvii–xxi). This technique is usually a profitable one when applied to Voltaire, and M. Pomeau himself has used it with considerable success in his edition of *Candide*.[3] Here, however, he may be trying to discover a similar focal point for this tale when that point may not exist. Of the sixteen resemblances he establishes, some are commonplaces in Voltaire's writings;[4] while others, as his own edition subsequently makes clear, do not appear in the first edition;[5] the explicit analogy with a letter of 9 March 1772 turns out, in the edition of it which has since been provided by Dr. Besterman, not to be correct, since the precise reference does not appear until Voltaire revised the letter for publication in 1776.[6] In other words, several pieces of evidence used by M. Pomeau are not at all localized in 1771–1772. Of those that remain, it is true that some, particularly those from the articles 'Enchantement' (1771) and 'Tolérance' (1772) of the *Questions sur l'Encyclopédie* provide an interesting cluster. But Voltaire may well be writing these passages with the complete first draft of *Le Taureau blanc* in mind, rather than the other way round; we know, for instance, that he often refers textually in his correspondence to *contes* like *Candide* after they have been completed. Furthermore, M. Pomeau's concentration upon the early 1770's ignores the considerable evidence in favour of an earlier date; and it may be well to look at this for a while before proceeding.

Already, in 1765, certain textual similarities are manifest. In the *Questions sur les miracles*, published in that year, Voltaire writes: 'Dieu . . . fait remonter le grand fleuve du Jourdain vers sa source, tomber les murs au son de la trompette, arrêter le soleil (et même la lune . . .).'[7] The first edition of *Le Taureau blanc* refers to all these acts: 'Josué qui fit tomber, au son du cornet, tous les murs de Jérico . . . arrêta le soleil et la lune . . .' (Pomeau ed., p. 48 n.). 'Je suis lasse . . . des fleuves qui montent à leur source . . .' (ibid., p. 52 and n.). The same *Questions sur les miracles* professes wonder that eight people could have catered for all the animals in Noah's Ark,[8] and refers to Manethon and his writings in connection with the dispute between Moses and the Egyptian magicians in miracle-making;[9] both these allusions are taken up in *Le Taureau blanc* (P. ed., pp. 36, 46), whose philosopher Mambrès had been one of those Egyptian wizards (ibid., n. 4, p. 68). These references are supported by allusions in Voltaire's correspondence during this period: to the walls of Jericho (Besterman 11505, 25 January 1765), to Elijah's chariot of fire (B. 11634, 20 March 1765), to the Israelites' derivativeness in matters of myth (B. 11672, 3 April 1765). Voltaire may have been influenced by a long letter received from Fabry de Moncault, who wrote to Voltaire on 1 July 1765 (B. 11930). This letter mentions Manethon as a writer on Moses, adds that 'les sages d'Egipte . . . adoraient des crocodiles et des chats' and attempts to defend the credibility of 'la longue vie des Patriarches'; all this is grist for Voltaire's mill. When Fabry writes: 'Il me paroit encore très évident que Moïse est beaucoup plus ancien qu'Homère et Hériode,' Voltaire notes in the margin: 'Ouy mais non pas que Zoroastre . . .' This latter point is stressed in *Le Taureau blanc*, when Mambrès refers to the antiquity of the Persian philosopher: 'comme disait autrefois mon maître Zoroastre' (P. ed., p. 38); and Voltaire adds another relevant note: 'Juifs ont pris . . . leurs cérémonies des Egiptiens.'

The similarities between *Le Taureau blanc* and Voltaire's other works, however, are not limited merely to 1765. A similar series of parallels can be drawn up for the following years. In *Le Douteur et l'adorateur*, which appeared in the *Recueil nécessaire*, published in 1766 (B. 12628, 25 August 1766), there are references to Balaam's ass, to the tale 'que Samson ait attaché ensemble trois cents renards par la queue'[10] (reproduced in similar phraseology in *Le Taureau blanc* (P. ed., p. 49)), to the paradox that God should have forbidden Adam and Eve the knowledge of good and evil which is so necessary to mankind[11] (another point taken up in similar terms in the *conte* (P. ed., p. 18)). The *Recueil nécessaire* also contained the *Examen de milord Bolingbroke*, where we find God bringing down the walls of Jericho 'au son du *cornet*',[12] the word used in *Le Taureau blanc* (P. ed., p. 48 n.). In 1766 too Voltaire receives a letter which may have had a seminal influence; it comes from Frederick II, the Landgrave of Hesse-Cassel:

J'ai fait depuis quelque tems des Réflexions sur Moise . . . Le Serpent d'Airin ne ressemble pas Mal, au Dieu Esculape, Les Cherubins au Sfincs, Les Bœufs qui étoient sous la Mer d'airin où Les Israelites faisoient Les Ablutions, au Dieu Apis. Enfin il paroit que Moise avoit donné à ce Peuple beaucoup de Cérémonies Religieuses qu'il avoit pris de La Religion des Egyptiens (B. 12754, 1 November 1766).

There are too many close points of comparison here with *Le Taureau blanc* for them all to be written off as pure coincidence, it would seem. And so perhaps it is not surprising to find Voltaire making one of his rare references to Nebuchadnezzar, the 'taureau blanc' himself, in a letter written some weeks later (B. 12875, [c. 25 December 1766]).

In early 1767, Voltaire voices one of his recurrent complaints about the contradictoriness of life[13] (cf: 'ce monde-ci subsiste de contradictions' (P. ed., p. 38)); and he is in a receptive mood to Catherine the Great's gibe about being deified and thereby put on the same footing as onions, cats, serpents, crocodiles and other animals (B. 12973, 20 January 1767), since he takes up the remark in letters to her[14] and others (B. 13098, 27 February 1767; 13100, 28 February 1767). There is a reference in another letter about this time (B. 13114, 3 March 1767), to animals reasoning with men, while in yet another the nostalgic regret for youth is sounded in a way reminiscent of the *conte*: 'Où est le tems où j'assistais à vos répétitions. . . . Hélas je suis trop vieux . . .'[15] (The snake in *Le Taureau blanc* sighs in similar fashion: 'J'aurais pu autrefois vous faire passer quelques quarts-d'heure assez agréables. . . . Hélas! où est le tems où j'amusais les filles!' (P. ed., p. 52)). In a letter of 11 March, Voltaire is seen to be giving close attention to 'les conquêtes de Josué', including an almost obligatory reference to the walls of Jericho and the arresting of sun and moon (B. 13132); these and other details relate closely to the first edition of the *conte* (P. ed., p. 48 n.). Finally, we should perhaps mention Voltaire's whimsical reference to the bulls he owned: 'Je vais déffendre à mes taureaux . . . de faire l'amour' in another letter from this period (B. 13224, 16 April [1767]).

At about this time Voltaire must have just completed *Les Questions de Zapata*, the first reference to which occurs in a letter of 4 March 1767 (B. 13115); here too there are textual likenesses. The work asks, *à propos* of the Tree of Knowledge: 'Voulait-il [Dieu] n'être servi que par un sot?'[16] *Le Taureau blanc* has the snake phrase the same question: 'Le maître aurait-il voulu être servi par des ignorans & des idiots?' (P. ed., p. 18). *Les Questions de Zapata*, furthermore, refers to the snake of the Garden of Eden, who has 'tant d'esprit',[17] another link with the imaginative structure of *Le Taureau blanc*. There are also allusions to Joshua's battle against the Amorites, Jephthah, Samson, Ezechiel, Aholibah, and the 'grand poisson' that swallowed Jonah.[18] Many of these are all too common in Voltaire's Biblical polemics, but here again the similarity in phraseology is sometimes striking.

It seems difficult, therefore, to resist the conclusion that *Le Taureau blanc* goes back to at least 1766–1767 and possibly earlier. It would even appear probable that the work was added to at intervals over the years, since certain key passages coincide so closely with references from particular periods. The *Instruction à Frère Pédiculoso* (1768–1769) adds one or two relevant details, such as the information that '*chérub* . . . en chaldéen signifie un bœuf',[19] which appears in the first edition of the *conte* in precisely these terms (P. ed., p. 6 n.), and the usual Biblical allusions to Ezechiel, Aholah and Aholibah, whose predilections Voltaire never tired of quoting; but the reference to Joshua's miracle regarding the sun and moon is more precise now, since it includes mention of Gibeon and Ajalon, which also appear in Chapter VIII of the tale (P. ed., p. 48 n.). Indeed, the *Instruction* has about it something of that disabused quality which in a gentler vein is also characteristic of *Le Taureau blanc*. It would seem as if the tale, unlike most of Voltaire's, grew by a process of crystallization. Upon the original framework details are deposited, like frost upon glass; the more marvellous or ludicrous items in the Old Testament find a double echo, in his polemics and in this work. And so, presumably, the story gathered substance, until there came the moment in 1772–1773 when, as M. Pomeau shows quite convincingly, Voltaire decided to proceed to a revision of the text.[20] At this point, as the editor demonstrates, a few references in other works seem to indicate a comprehensive awareness of at least certain passages; but there are also earlier periods when similar configurations appear, so numerous and dense at times as to suggest that Voltaire momentarily had the *conte* very much in mind.

Perhaps, then, we have been too ready to assume that this was Voltaire's swan song. In its final form it may be so, but the original inspiration should be advanced by several years in Voltaire's life. And this may be a desirable modification, for it would place *Le Taureau blanc* in the same creative period as *L'Ingénu*, instead of assigning it to the exhausted limbo after all the great works have been completed and thereby seeming to damn it with faint praise. We do not need to take Voltaire's implicit professions of declining powers as firm evidence for the 1770's; such assertions are not at all uncommon a decade earlier, while the old man is at the same time producing the myriad 'mélanges', plays and *contes* which this period sees appear.

'A *conte philosophique*,' says W. F. Bottiglia, 'is a stylized demonstration.'[21] The remark holds as true for *Le Taureau blanc* as for any other of Voltaire's tales. In the *Sermon des cinquante*, he had long before dismissed the Old Testament stories as 'contes';[22] the whole polemical intention of this tale is to reinforce that view.[23] Eventually, the point is made explicitly by the princess Amaside who, for all her sweet gentleness, is irritated by the snake's endless tales of improbable and odious incidents in the Old Testament:

> Tous ces contes-là m'ennuient, répondit la belle *Amaside*, qui avait de l'esprit & du goût. Ils ne sont bons que pour être commentés chez les Irlandais par ce fou d'*Abadie*, ou chez les Welches par ce phrasier d'*Houteville*. Les contes qu'on pouvait faire à la quadrisayeule de la quadrisayeule de ma grand'mère, ne sont plus bons pour moi qui ai été élevée par le sage *Mambrès*, & qui ai lu l'*entendement humain* du philosophe égyptien nommé *Locke*, & la *matrone d'Ephèse*. Je veux qu'un conte soit fondé sur la vraisemblance, & qu'il ne ressemble pas toûjours à un rêve. Je désire qu'il n'ait rien de trivial ni d'extravagant. Je voudrais surtout que, sous le voile de la fable, il laissât entrevoir aux yeux exercés

quelque vérité fine qui échappe au vulgaire. Je suis lasse du soleil & de la lune dont une vieille dispose à son gré, des montagnes qui dansent, des fleuves qui remontent à leur source, & des morts qui ressuscitent; mais surtout, quand ces fadaises sont écrites d'un style ampoulé et inintelligible, cela me dégoûte horriblement (P. ed., pp. 51–52).

Here Voltaire clearly, perhaps too clearly, distinguishes between a *conte* and a *conte philosophique*. This aim had already been manifest in the ironic stylization. The work begins as an apparently straightforward fairy tale. Nothing in the first paragraph suggests any ambiguous intention, except the mildly surprising remark about Amaside that 'on sait quel était le sujet de sa douleur', when it is clear that we have no such knowledge at all. The next paragraph, however, jolts us into awareness of the Voltairean approach: 'La princesse était âgée de vingt-quatre ans. Le mage *Mambrès* en avait environ treize cent.' Reality and fantasy are inextricably mingled. More precise and penetrating irony is quickly to follow. Mambrès is connected with Moses; they once had had 'cette dispute fameuse, dans laquelle la victoire fut longtemps balancée entre ces deux profonds philosophes'. It sounds like a learned disputation; Leibniz and Bayle, or Voltaire himself and Pascal, might come naturally to the contemporary reader's mind. But it is none of this. The victory was not determined by reasoned discourse, but by crude divine intervention: 'Si *Mambrès* succomba, ce ne fut que par la protection visible des puissances célestes qui favorisèrent son rival; il fallut des Dieux pour vaincre *Mambrès*.' And so it becomes clear; we are in a magical world, a world where enlightenment cannot prevail before supernatural power; furthermore, although set in Egypt, it is already clear that the Old Testament is the target. From these fragmentary indications in the opening paragraphs the picture will quickly develop. We soon find ourselves in the presence of the Witch of Endor, Balaam's ass, the 'gros poisson' that swallowed Jonah, and similar diverting but wholly absurd characters. Not least among them is the beautiful white bull whose identity Voltaire will gradually reveal: it is Nebuchadnezzar, transformed precisely as the Biblical prediction had said he would be. Out of that enigmatic prophecy, so baffling for commentators down the centuries (P. ed., n. 21, pp. 74–77), Voltaire has constructed the essential framework of his story.

The absurdities are heightened at every point. The magic is not merely ubiquitous, it is wholly arbitrary. Why can the snake and the ass speak so well when the noble bull cannot, Amaside sadly wonders (P. ed., p. 11). Voltaire makes fine play with the opportunities afforded him by these humanized animals, and one is inevitably reminded of La Fontaine as a possible influence.[24] (He had in any case long since been compared to his illustrious predecessor by Cardinal de Bernis and Cideville as a writer of *contes*.[25]) Be that as it may, Voltaire heaps one ludicrous juxtaposition upon another. The snake not only has eyes both 'tendres' and 'animés'; 'sa physionomie était noble & intéressante' (P. ed., p. 4), and Amaside herself later dwells upon this incongruity ('la finesse de votre physionomie' (P. ed., p. 16)) as one of the traits encouraging her to seek his advice. If Voltaire makes play with such improbabilities, it is because they are directly related to the world of the Old Testament. Here is a universe of incessant nonsensicality, a world where eight people care for thousands of animals in the Ark on a seemingly inexhaustible supply of food (P. ed., pp. 36–37), where the doings of Aholah and Aholibah are merely 'fleurs de réthorique',[26] where somehow you can discharge all your sins upon a 'bouc émissaire' by sending him out into the desert—'l'on sait que tout s'expie avec un bouc qui se promène' (P. ed., p. 31). Not for Voltaire the comparative anthropologist's view which might make sense of such absurdities; to his rationalist mind all this was the manifestation of Anti-Reason and should be exposed as such. Metamorphoses come naturally in this unnatural world: 'On ne marchait dans mon jeune tems que sur des métamorphoses', says Mambrès (P. ed., p. 28). So it is logical that he should succeed with his own stratagem at the end: '*Daniel* a changé cet homme en bœuf, & j'ai changé ce bœuf en Dieu' (P. ed., p. 63), he remarks, revealing that *pince sans rire* humour which fits his character so well. Such a setting is well suited to the Biblical prophets Daniel, Ezechiel and Jeremiah, who are not at all the charismatic leaders of the Palestinian Jews but instead the pathetic, filthy, ragged, half-starved wretches that Voltaire imagines them to have been, their only extraordinary attribute being not prophetic vision but simply the fanatic's arrogance (P. ed., pp. 38–44). His final comment on them is to turn them, suitably enough, into three loquacious magpies (P. ed., p. 44).

This world is not only nonsensical; the rest of humanity has never even heard of it. One need not labour this point, which Voltaire makes frequently, here and elsewhere (P. ed., n. 15, pp. 71–72), beyond indicating how it is on occasion reduced to a neat ironic paradox, as with 'l'arche de Noé, grand événement, catastrophe universelle, que presque toute la terre ignore encore' (P. ed., p. 9), or Amaside's mention of Eve, 'notre mère commune dont j'ai oublié le nom' (P. ed., p. 18). Here in essence is the world-view of the *Essai sur les moeurs* liquidating that of the *Discours sur l'histoire universelle*. Bossuet's vision centres precisely upon this one particular and tiny race, for to him they are chosen of God, while to Voltaire, that unique quality removed, they are no more than a petty, primitive and unlovely tribe.[27] But it is above all the myth of Eve and the Garden of Eden which comes in for particular attack. For not only is this largely unknown in the outside world and in any case adapted from the much greater civilization of India; it does not add up to common sense. Surely God would want his children to be as enlightened as possible? If not, why plant a Tree of Knowledge in their domain? The snake was convinced that he was helping humanity by advising Eve to eat (P. ed., pp. 15–18). After a lifetime's tussle with the problem of evil, Voltaire remains bewildered and ignorant of any explanation that offers him satisfaction. But of one thing he is certain; the Garden of Eden theory is totally misconceived.

Even now we have not penetrated to the heart of Voltaire's objections to the Old Testament. This age is superstitious and parochial, but it is odious as well as absurd, for it condones persecution and massacre. Voltaire does not fail to refer frequently to such examples as the 'héros' Joshua whose prodigious feats are all directed to killing and destruction, or 'les avantures du grand *Samson*' (P. ed., pp. 48–49), equally barbarous and horrible. More interestingly, however, he builds this element into the structure of his story, investing Amaside's father, King Amasis, with the odium one should feel for all such characters. Amasis has the monomania of Voltaire's best caricatures. For him, a king has the right, indeed the obligation, to be wrathful and to kill his daughter even though he professes to love her.[28] When she transgresses his commandment, then it becomes a straightforward judicial matter: 'Il est juste que je vous coupe le cou' (P. ed., p. 58). The ridiculous nature of her transgression (she has uttered the name of her beloved Nebuchadnezzar) only heightens the cruelty. Old Testament justice is seen as legalistic, not moral, based on punishment, not love. It is easy to discern behind Amasis the cruel Jehovah of the Israelites, than whom no more abhorrent view of God could be imagined by Voltaire, as M. Pomeau's *La Religion de Voltaire*[29] so clearly demonstrates. Indeed, Amasis must carry out his punishment, 'sans quoi il est précipité pour jamais dans les enfers, & je ne veux pas me damner pour l'amour de vous' (P. ed., p. 63). In such a horrible world, the creatures of this terrible God must destroy one another for their creator's pleasure.

Despite these indictments, Voltaire approaches all these abominations with a calm urbanity that pervades the whole tale. The irony is usually attenuated, scarcely ever savage. There is no need for pyrotechnics in dealing with these targets, so ridiculous are they. Voltaire's prayer, he once wrote, was very brief: 'Mon Dieu, rendez nos ennemis bien ridicules!' He adds with satisfaction, 'Dieu m'a exaucé' (B. 13287, 16 May 1767). Here there is scarcely any call to raise his voice. Elijah goes up to Heaven in a chariot of fire, 'quoique ce ne soit pas la coutume' (P. ed., p. 35). Voltaire speaks of the sacred onions of the Egyptian priests 'qui n'étaient pas tout-à-fait des Dieux, mais qui leur ressemblaient beaucoup' (P. ed., p. 60). The absurdity requires no elucidation, just the merest exposure in the ironic mirror.

Through this crazy world moves one wise man, Mambrès. He

is, like Voltaire, a 'vieux solitaire'[30] and past his prime; he too lives
in a 'désert', a 'pays barbare' (B. 14844, 16 August [1769]). He must
sadly confess: 'ma science baisse à mesure que mon âge avance'
(P. ed., p. 14); the point is made over and over again from at least the
1760's on by a Voltaire who feels the onset of age (e.g., B. 13020, 4
February 1767). If we find Mambrès 'toûjours faisant des réflexions' (P. ed., p. 38), he merely echoes Voltaire writing in his
letters to Mme Du Deffand: 'j'ai passé tout mon temps à méditer'
(B. 12307, 19 February 1766), and a little later that she is, like him,
in her old age and 'précisément dans l'état où l'on fait des réflexions'
(B. 12333, 12 March 1766); it is simply rather more so for his correspondent since she is blind as well. 'Le discret *Mambrès*' (P. ed.,
p. 41) resembles his author, who asserts that 'dans un temps de
persécution, il faut opposer la discrétion à la méchanceté des
hommes' (B. 12695, 22 September [1766]). He is kind, helpful,
persuasive, prudent, a man better than his environment; in all these
attributes the self-identification is clear. Like Voltaire, he is a sage,
convinced that this is at bottom a world of contradictions.[31] But
his author is not disposed merely to make of Mambrès a mouth-
piece. Like other heroes, such as the Ingénu, the magician will
serve a dual function, portraying Voltairean attitudes but also,
because he is an objective figure set in a totally un-Voltairean time,
representing a point of view which Voltaire holds up to mockery.
In the original version of the tale, Mambrès is introduced in much
more admiring terms:

L'âge affaiblit cette tête si supérieure aux autres têtes, & cette
puissance qui avait résisté à la puissance universelle; mais il lui
resta toujours un grand fond de raison; il ressemblait à ces im-
menses bâtiments de l'antique Egypte dont les ruines attestent la
grandeur. Mambrès était encore fort bon pour le conseil, &
quoiqu'un peu vieux, il avait l'âme très compatissante (P. ed.,
p. 2 n.).

All this is unsubtle eulogy, and, quite rightly, excised from the later
editions. In consequence, Voltaire's manner from the first is bene-
volent, but detached. 'Le sage Mambrès' is also 'le grand mage

D

Mambrès' (P. ed., p. 25), 'divin mage! divin eunuque!' (P. ed., p. 6). His heroic stature is partly Voltairean, but it is also sometimes purely Biblical. For he often speaks and acts like an Old Testament prophet, and in that rôle he is useless, he is a prophet who cannot even prophesy: 'Je ne sais pas ce qu'on fera de vos autres bêtes, car tout prophète que je suis, je sais bien peu de choses . . .' (P. ed., p. 30). In his prophet-like moods, he asserts that only 'un ordre de la Providence universelle' can account for his encounter with the Witch of Endor, and pours scorn upon the 'faux sages' in the generations to come who will disbelieve his and her miracles (P. ed., pp. 8, 10). At such moments, the 'faux sage' Voltaire makes his presence felt; here essentially lies the reason for a portrayal that, judged on purely psychological grounds, has a fundamental inconsistency in it.

Such an inconsistency is not confined to Mambrès; it is shared by the snake, though his rôle is of lesser importance. On the one hand he is the urbane gentleman, gallant towards women and yet doomed to get them, through no fault of his own, into trouble. On one level he too is Voltaire, hoping to charm but finding it increasingly difficult. We have already seen that his remark: 'Hélas! où est le tems où j'amusais les filles!' is a *cri de coeur* echoed in Voltaire's correspondence. The old man will write to the marquis de Saint-Lambert: 'Je suis un vieillard très galant avec les Dames . . . (B. 17442, 1 September 1773); but nearly a decade before he has already had to admit: 'Il m'est impossible de parler à une jeune femme plus d'un demi quart d'heure' (B. 11103, 20 June 1764). Such is the pathos behind the snake's boring tales; but there is another dimension. These stories are boring because they are not Voltairean *contes*, but merely Biblical ones. Voltaire adroitly separates himself from his creation, albeit sympathetically. The snake serves a further purpose. As the supposed Devil who charmed Eve he has some ominous statements to make: 'J'oserais presque dire que toute la terre m'appartient' (P. ed., p. 17). Mambrès, in perhaps his most philosophical speech, wonders how the snake holds so much power, and admits that the question is beyond him (P. ed., p. 38). As we have seen, Voltaire is merely expressing his old dilemma on this subject and showing his contempt for the Judaeo-Christian explanation. But here too the characterization is psychologically unsatisfactory, and derives its full meaning only from its *philosophique* import.

For, as always, it is Voltaire who is present in the forefront throughout. 'Je est un conte', Yvon Belaval puts it neatly.[32] All the other characters are the flimsiest of creations. Amaside is the conventional heroine, frail, tender, gracious, submissive, though Voltaire realistically grants her a normal young woman's libido (P. ed., p. 12) and allows her emancipation in the final triumph, when the natural code of life at last defeats the supernatural. The animals, apart from the snake, are a motley collection, with only the odd capricious trait to distinguish them, like the heartlessness of the 'gros poisson' or the crow's gluttony; and even this latter quality is used only to launch an attack on the Noah's Ark legend. It is Voltaire's voice which is raised on high above them all, Voltaire whose versatility of style, comprehensively explored by M. Pomeau (P. ed., pp. xlviii–lxxii), reminds us constantly of the artist at work. The jolting anachronisms prevent us from ever suspending our disbelief. Amaside has read Locke (P. ed., p. 51), the snake refers to Milton's *Paradise Lost* (P. ed., p. 17), Mambrès' dignified letter contains a direct anticipation of the *Venite adoremus* of Christ's Nativity (P. ed., p. 33). If Voltaire writes: 'On conclut à la pluralité des voix qu'il falait exorciser la princesse, & sacrifier le taureau blanc & la vieille' (P. ed., p. 25), he has in mind the system of French criminal justice, where a man like Calas can be condemned to death on a simple majority vote. Mambrès' simple remark: 'ce n'est que par des contes qu'on réussit dans le monde' (P. ed., p. 46) reminds us of the perplexed Voltaire whose tales were best-sellers, while his carefully-worked tragedies like *Les Scythes* and *Les Lois de Minos* were received with indifference. This *conte* is as totally Voltairean as any, less profound than some but in the first rank by its freshness and charm. The 'instabilité d'humeur' of which M. Pomeau writes in his edition of *Candide*[33] has disappeared. What remains is sympathy for human beings when they are truly human: the young

lovers at all times, the snake when he ceases to embody an out-
moded myth and represents only himself, Mambrès when he is not a
seer but a natural old man. It is the same plea as ever from Voltaire:
forget systems and ideologies, banish transcendental nonsense,
concentrate on a practical morality based upon personal liberty and
happiness. At the end Nebuchadnezzar's people cry out with delight:
'Vive notre grand roi qui n'est plus bœuf!' The pun is neatly
deflationary, in contrast to all the grandiose falsity of Amasis and the
priests; and it reminds us that what counts more than all these
marvellous and fairy-tale metamorphoses is the reality of human
happiness, supported and encouraged by the conduct of a good and
wise king. Norman Suckling ends a recent article on this same note,
referring to Professor Torrey's notion of progress, the only valid one,
'that man has nothing to hope for . . . from any power other than his
own.'[34]

H. T. MASON

REFERENCES

1 Paris, Nizet, 1956.
2 *Voltaire's Correspondence*, Ed. Besterman, Geneva, Institut et Musée Voltaire, 1953–1965, 107 vols., (hereafter referred to as B.), letter no. 17050.
3 Paris, Nizet, 1959.
4 Voltaire refers to the 'bouc émissaire' (Pomeau ed., p. xviii, n. 35) quite often (cf. e.g., B. 12377, 13 April 1766; B. 15088, 5 January 1770); the proverbial prudence of the serpent (Pomeau ed., p. xviii, n. 39) likewise appears regularly (cf. B. 13212, 13 April 1767; B. 13433, 3 August 1767). (Hereafter Pomeau is referred to as P. ed.)
5 The 'déluge de Xissutre' (p. xvii); the quotations from St. Irenaeus and Tertullian (ibid.), and from the Book of Kings (p. xviii); the textual analogies regarding Amphion (ibid.).
6 Cf. B. 16583 and app. 256.
7 *Œuvres complètes*, Ed. L. Moland, Paris, Garnier, 1877–1885, 52 vols. (hereafter referred to as M.), XXV, p. 434.
8 M., XXV, p. 443.
9 Ibid., p. 411.
10 M., XXV, p. 134.
11 Ibid.
12 M., XXVI, p. 211; my underlining.
13 B. 12936, 10 January 1767. The letter is actually written by Mme Denis, but the editor points out that most of it was undoubtedly dictated by Voltaire.
14 B. 13097, 27 February 1767; this letter adds a reference to the 'bœuf Apis', not mentioned by Catherine. Cf. P. ed., p. 33.

15 B. 13040, 10 February 1767; the phrase 'où est le temps . . .' recurs in
    B. 13231, 19 April 1767.
16 M., XXVI, p. 175.
17 Ibid., cf. 'Il [le serpent] a de l'esprit', P. ed., p. 14.
18 M., XXVI, pp. 179–184.
19 M., XXVII, p. 302; the point has, however, already been made in a
    rather less close parallel in Les Questions de Zapata, M., XXVI, p. 175.
20 In a letter of 4 December 1772 to Voltaire, Frederick II of Prussia
    reports that when he asked the Director of his Porcelain Factory why he
    had decorated a bowl and coffee cup sent to Voltaire with the figure of
    Amphion, the Director had linked Amphion to Voltaire: 'si Amphion
    avait par ses sons harmonieux élevé les murs de Thèbes, il connaissait
    quelqu'un vivant qui en avait fait davantage' (B. 16999). Amphion does
    not appear in the first edition of Le Taureau blanc, but he comes into
    all the later versions as a positive counterpart to the odiously destructive
    Joshua (P. ed., pp. 48–49); and the reference is such as to suggest a link
    between Frederick's letter and Voltaire's revision. This would point to
    Voltaire's working on Le Taureau blanc either at or shortly after mid-
    December. It must however be added that Voltaire had already estab-
    lished a direct contrast between Amphion and Joshua in the Examen
    de milord Bolingbroke (1766), M., XXVI, p. 211; so the matter must
    remain unresolved.
21 'Voltaire's Candide: Analysis of a Classic', Studies on Voltaire and the
    Eighteenth Century, VII A (1964), p. 74.
22 M., XXIV, pp. 446–447.
23 For a thorough discussion of Voltaire's views on the Old Testament as
    set forth in his polemical works, cf. two articles by A. Ages, 'Voltaire's
    Biblical Criticism: A Study in Thematic Repetitions', Studies on
    Voltaire, XXX (1964), pp. 205–221; 'Voltaire, Calmet and the Old
    Testament', ibid., XLI (1966), pp. 87–187.
24 Is it entirely coincidental to find Voltaire alluding to La Fontaine when
    working on the final version in 1773? Cf. B. 17042, 17105, 17139,
    17221, 17250.
25 B. 10925, 11 March 1764; 10994, 17 April 1764. One must however
    point out that the occasion is the appearance of a verse rather than a
    prose conte by Voltaire, Les Trois Manières.
26 P. ed., p. 43. Voltaire has little love at any time for allegorical interpreta-
    tions of the Bible.
27 Cf. J. H. Brumfitt ed., La Philosophie de l'histoire, Studies on Voltaire,
    XXVIII (1963), pp. 30–33.
28 P. ed., p. 3: 'Vous savez que le roi votre père, qui d'ailleurs vous aime,
    a juré de vous faire couper le cou . . .'.
29 Paris, Nizet, 1956.
30 Cf. e.g., B. 13899, 14 March [1768]. But Mambrès at least can look back
    upon 1300 years of existence, whereas for Voltaire life is nearly over in
    his 70's.
31 P. ed., p. 38. Cf. e.g., B. 17105, 1 February 1773: 'Ce monde cy est plein
    de contradictions . . .'.
32 'L'Esprit de Voltaire', Studies on Voltaire, XXIV (1963), p. 147.
33 Op. cit., p. 61.
34 'The Enlightenment and the Idea of Progress', Studies on Voltaire,
    LVIII (1967), p. 1480.

TABLEAUX MOUVANTS AS A TECHNICAL INNOVATION IN DIDEROT'S EXPERIMENTAL NOVEAL, *JACQUES LE FATALISTE*

Diderot's dramatic theories have been studied from various standpoints. They have been situated in their historical and social context, and judged solely valid in terms of the plays enacted during the second half of the eighteenth century. Some critics have pointed to more distant influence on the evolution of melodrama and romantic drama; others have been concerned to show how Diderot has anticipated Scribe, Augier and Dumas *fils*, writers who discussed social, moral or philosophical issues in their plays, and suggested that a conflict of ideas may prove as dramatic as the interplay of human passions. More recently, attention has been paid to Diderot's views on the role of scenic design; to his general conception of the theatre, including the function, psychology and status of the actor, the nature and size of the theatre itself, and its suitability for the type of performance and type of public for which it is ostensibly designed. More attention might have been given to his emphasis on *l'unité de discours* in a given play, which brings out the importance of the playwright, and lends a new significance to the *guida maestro* of Italian Comedy, now becoming a true *producer* in the modern meaning of the word. Diderot's two *drames*, *Le Père de Famille* and *Le Fils Naturel*, are now little else but museum-pieces of interest to historians generally, and more especially to those of the theatre. Few critics, in fact, have seen the full significance of the *drames*, the new form of bourgeois theatre halfway between tragedy and comedy, as a vital step in the direction of greater realism. Erich Auerbach in *Mimesis* has made valuable references to the *comédie larmoyante*, but his subsequent conclusions would have been even more securely based had he included *le drame* by name in his detailed analysis. In an early chapter he had referred to the 'seclusion and isolation' of the tragic process resting on a very complicated and multi-layered tradition; one, moreover, that is highly artificial and can only be seen as reasonable in terms of its own perspective. From this point of view, classical and Italian comedy, as well as classical tragedy, stand condemned. Much further on in his conclusion, he states:

They [the realist novelists of the nineteenth century, especially Balzac and Stendhal] broke with the classical rule of distinct levels of style, for according to this rule, everyday practical reality could find a place in literature only within the frame of a low or intermediate kind of style, that is to say, as either grotesquely comic or pleasant, light, colorful, and elegant entertainment. They thus completed a development which had long been in preparation (since the time of the novel of manners and the *comédie larmoyante* of the XVIIIth century, and more pronouncedly since the *Sturm und Drang* and early romanticism). And they opened the way for modern realism, which has ever since developed in increasingly rich forms, in keeping with the constantly changing and expanding reality of modern life.[1]

Whatever its failings, the *drame*, which incorporates the *comédie larmoyante*, provided a milestone in this evolution; and its influence, bifurcating into romanticism on the one hand, and realism on the other, can clearly be discerned. These two main currents grew ever more apart as the nineteenth century proceeded, but met again in the twentieth, when fantasy and realism were no longer seen as necessarily exclusive.

One noteworthy feature in Auerbach's analysis is that he has stressed, not the role of the novel, but that of the theatre in the development of realism. When we turn specifically to Diderot, we find likewise that Y. Belaval[2] has sought the basis of the author's aesthetic in his writings on the theatre, and in his plays. In the following essay we shall be concerned with one particular and most important aspect of Diderot's technique for the expression of reality, his use of *tableaux*, which developed from a theatrical device into an essential element of a new kind of realism.

Diderot's theory of *drame* is based on a general philosophy of nature, involving the deepening of his original concept of art as an imitation of nature. He saw the need to convey at least the illusion of reality when writing for the stage, and to this end he deemed best to present men who are not perpetually in a state of grief or joy, who live ordinary lives, who have a family and a profession. The *drame*, as he envisaged it, was therefore to be a serious, and not a frivolous, comment on contemporary society. Given the axiom that the theatre lends itself to all forms of art which make a special appeal to the senses, Diderot welcomed the possible creation of hybrid forms, mixing the resources of plastic art, *tableaux*, décors, mime, gesture and voice. In his writings, in search of an increased range of theatrical experience and truth, he anticipated grand opera, romantic ballet and the use of simultaneous sets. In his *Entretiens sur le Fils Naturel* he stressed the need for *tableaux*, or stage pictures, to enhance the realism, and for actors to behave naturally on the stage.

These *tableaux* held great potentiality for conveying facile emotion. He wrote: 'Il y a des scènes entières où il est infiniment plus naturel aux personnages de se mouvoir que de parler';[3] and saw the importance of gesture and movement, and that unfinished sentences, exclamations and the like could convey emotion; but he realized even more clearly that a lasting impression could be made by visual emphasis even better than by words. *Pantomime* itself is 'le tableau qui existait dans l'imagination du poète, lorsqu'il écrivait; et qu'il voudrait que la scène montrât à chaque instant lorsqu'on le joue'.[4] Diderot had a visual imagination, as M. T. Cartwright has demonstrated.[5] Yet the scenes in *Le Père de Famille* and *Le Fils Naturel* proved to be dramatically unsuccessful, partly because they brought the action to a standstill. But his conception of the theatre as essentially a spectacle, and more generally his visual imagination, his desire for a realistic décor to replace the old, conventional settings, and his sense of the potentialities for effective scene-shifting once the stage had been cleared of spectators, were transposed into a new literary form, as evidenced in his novels. His failure with his plays is perhaps due to an erroneous conception of what is natural on the stage. His formalized compositions did not create the illusion of life,

D*

and in no wise heightened the reality of the action. His appeal to the emotions was too facile and his *tirades*, full of moral disquisitions or explanatory notes, did not allow for the necessary concentration of character and dramatic action. Characterization and dialogue, décor and attitudes are all set in a fixed pattern which cannot be expected to move the spectator.

The general theory, however, had validity and remained present in Diderot's mind. The importance in his eyes of *tableaux* and *pantomime*, and his view of the theatre, as of life itself, as a spectacle, led him to use in his novels what was an essentially dramatic technique, one whose latent possibilities he was eager to explore. The influence of Richardson's novels has often been stressed, for they helped him to crystallize his ideas on realism. These novels certainly provided him with examples of *tragédies bourgeoises* with an unwonted emphasis on detailed description of physical and psychological traits, so as to heighten overall realism. Diderot wrote:

> Une des principales différences du roman domestique et du drame c'est que le roman suit le geste et la pantomime dans tous leurs détails; que l'auteur s'attache principalement à peindre et les mouvements et les impressions; au lieu que le poète dramatique n'en jette qu'un mot en passant.[6]

The novel in fact provided him with greater scope for mingling narrative, dialogue and *tableaux*.

In *La Religieuse* attitudes are no longer subordinated to speech, as in most novels. Emotional distress, for instance, is at various moments conveyed by images such as 'renversée sur une chaise'. But many of the gestures remain theatrical, the stances adopted seem exaggerated and static, so as to affect more assuredly the audience or the reader. Diderot takes trouble to portray accurately facial expression and clothing, the outward manifestations of anger or pain. If the attitudes taken by his characters are frozen as in some *tableau vivant* or a painting by Greuze, the scenes of dramatic dialogue and pathos are heightened by a sombre background, fitfully lit, which conveys a sense of horror and terror. By breaking a sequence of movement and making his character hold a given position Diderot succeeds in pinpointing it, and the emphasis created by this duration of description is of considerable advantage to the pictorial aspect of the *tableaux*, enabling the reader to visualize each scene very clearly. Thus when Suzanne describes a scene:

> Ma compagne priait droite; moi, je me prosternai; mon front était appuyé contre la dernière marche de l'autel, et mes bras étendus sur les marches supérieures . . . je fus un spectacle bien touchant, il le faut croire, pour ma compagne et pour les deux religieuses qui survinrent,[7]

the vivid quality of the description which matches the strong emotion is far more effective than comparable passages in the *drames*. Diderot's *tableaux pathétiques* have greater consistency and linger on in one's memory. The question of the purpose which is to be served, that of time and duration, are all important here. *La Religieuse* is essentially a sequence of touching and horrific scenes conveyed in the language of the theatre, accompanied by facial expressions, gestures, lighting effects, and décor, such as we should expect to find on the stage; but in this novel all are successfully used, since they truly form a dramatic and harmonious ensemble.

In the *Neveu de Rameau*, visual effects are also used to great advantage, as a background to the dialogue from which they often seem to spring. In this work Diderot exploited more particularly the artistic possibility of combining dialogue and *pantomime*, and the degree of integration realized is remarkable. The earlier, mostly static *tableaux* have here become animated; and descriptions of moving scenes show a quickening of tempo at a moment of climax or dramatic intensity. A combination of stylistic and pictorial skills infuses his *tableaux* with life so that they therefore make good theatre, for they are an outward manifestation of genuine emotion and of temperament, and they hold our interest through their constant mobility. This was at once apparent when *Le Neveu de Rameau* was successfully staged recently without any major modification of the text. If we examine closely Diderot's language, more especially his changes of tense from present to past, we discover that *tableaux vivants* go beyond the usual boundaries of visual expression, so often limited to gesture. In these *tableaux vivants*, the long descriptive passages do not impede the action, for they are concerned with the portrayal of the Nephew's gesticulations, which convey to us the core of his individuality. They help to build up realistically and convincingly both his personality and his artistic nature. There are at least twelve scenes of *pantomime* of varying length, which are indicative of the character and way of life of Rameau's Nephew. He is shown as a man who at times is estranged from himself, and whose identity is inseparable from his acts. The *tableaux vivants* are an integral part of the self-expression of the artist. They fit into a general choreography, and in his *pantomime* which has a balletic core Rameau's Nephew interprets the music of his soul through the action of his body in a specialized technique of movement. The fusion of sight, sound, intellect and sensibility is translated into words, but the quality of the vision, the impression left upon the mind, is that of a visual form of art. The quality of the vision, with its pictorial emphasis, reflects the development of Diderot's creative faculty in an increasingly individual and dramatic presentation, which owes little to the traditional novel form.

Jacques le Fataliste is Diderot's last experiment in literary form and artistic realism. Narration and dialogue, description and stage directions are intermingled. The numerous digressions involving the characters, the reader, and the author, fall into a discernible pattern with overall regard to verisimilitude. We find, rather than an imitation of reality, a recreation of it by means of a varied and essentially dramatic presentation. The possibilities for dramatization were realized as early as 1796 and 1812; in particular, the episode of Mme de La Pommeraye, and that of Jacques and Denise, were early adapted to the stage. The use of interruptions and digressions, which maintain an atmosphere of suspense, and of dialogue with a characteristic typographical layout, reinforce the impression that one is dealing with a dramatic production. Some of the descriptive notes provided by the author, such as 'en frappant sur sa tabatière et en regardant à sa montre l'heure qu'il est', and others given in parenthesis, may be likened to stage directions.

Many of the sketches have the pictorial quality of the *tableaux* we find in *La Religieuse*. Thus Mlle d'Aisnon at the feet of the Marquis des Arcis: 'Elle était échevelée; elle avait le corps un peu penché, les bras portés de son côté, la tête relevée, le regard attaché sur ses yeux, et le visage inondé de pleurs'.[8] This is an 'arrested shot' which holds the scene briefly, giving it a momentary emphasis before the action is allowed to continue: yet the overall impression is one of mobility.

Such *tableaux mouvants* record the actions or succession of scenes without any comment by the author. As in *Le Neveu de Rameau*, the accumulative structures and repetitions of words, ideas and movements are coupled with a passage from the past to the present tense in moments of excitement, and when there is a need to foster the illusion of immediacy. A detailed study of the long and vivid scene in the *Grand Cerf* would bear this out. The whole episode consists of a series of *tableaux mouvants*, which are the very antithesis of the still *tableaux*. Their use often serves a quickening-up process, and variations in tempo accompany the movements observed and conveyed visually. The change to the present tense in these *tableaux mouvants* may be likened to the 'close-up' in modern cinematographic technique, as in the following passage:

L'hôtesse ... se lève, entreprend Jacques, porte ses deux poings sur ses deux côtés, oublie qu'elle tient Nicole, la lâche, et voilà Nicole sur le carreau, froissée et se débattant dans son maillot, aboyant à tue-tête, l'hôtesse mêlant ses cris aux aboiements de Nicole, Jacques mêlant ses éclats de rire aux aboiements de Nicole et aux cris de l'hôtesse et le maître de Jacques ouvrant sa tabatière, reniflant sa prise de tabac et ne pouvant s'empêcher de rire. Voilà toute l'hôtellerie en tumulte.[9]

When, on the other hand, Diderot again reverts to the past tense, the reader–spectator draws away from the scene and the vision becomes less intense. It will readily be seen that the temporal and the pictorial aspects of the *tableaux* are closely linked. The sequence of time is often deliberately illogical, and even more significant than the visual quality. It is this peculiar use of time, seen as an essential element of description, that renders Diderot's presentation more complex and sophisticated than in his previous works. It also allows the author to gain far greater control over the working of illusion, which can now be conjured up or destroyed at will. The world Diderot is showing us is of his own creation, and therefore capricious; and it stretches realism to its utmost limits. By breaking down the usual artistic conventions of the novel and the theatre in this way, he is able to give life to his characters in a world outside space and time in which the disjointed pattern of events is reflected in ceaseless interruptions. If the characters are convincing, it is not through some *tour de force* of the author, but as the result of a well-considered technique. His time sequences and differing visual effects are evidence of a great intellectual and literary development in his original theatrical technique. Both Rameau's Nephew and Jacques and his Master hold their audience under their spell.

But in *Jacques le Fataliste* Diderot has moved beyond what can be called a stage production to a global recreation of life and movement, whilst still basically writing in terms of drama. Reference to modern fictional and cinematographic devices may help us to understand better what Diderot was really doing. Diderot's technique of alienating an audience from the action finds its modern counterpart in the theatre of Brecht, but this feeling of alienation—the word used by Diderot—or estrangement is more easily and commonly realized in the cinema through the skilful cutting of the editor. In a similar manner Diderot breaks the sequence of events and blots them out with another, or creates an interlude by chatting with the interlocutor. His mastery is that of the film director who knows when to cut, how far to allow a particular episode to be concluded before bringing in the next, when to transfer attention from one place to another to sustain a sense of excitement or suspense. Several *tableaux* in *Jacques le Fataliste* are like arrested shots, and provide a lull after which the action may be resumed. The cessation of movement then focusses attention on some significant detail, close-ups such as Mlle d'Aisnon kneeling, make wordless reactions more telling than dialogue would have been. But the *tableaux mouvants* lead to acceleration of the action and correspond to the fast motion technique of film, contrasting obviously with the immobility of the arrested shot. Scenes of frenzied action, such as that of pandemonium in the *Grand Cerf*, are reminiscent of wild chases in early comedy films, and Diderot achieves in language what has been considered the final expression of the motion picture medium—the pictorial elaboration of inter-related movements whose rapidity is essential to its visual impact. *Jacques* follows procedures of cutting and mixing sequences and producing unusual visual effects. A comparison between *Le Neveu de Rameau* and *Jacques le Fataliste* brings out the dissimilarity between stage and screen. In *Jacques le Fataliste* the selective method for building up the action is what is called in the cinema *montage*. As a director, Diderot limits the view to his own vision, or presents it in the desired perspective: but the overall impression on the spectator is that of the continuity of life, through the peregrinations of the characters, their stories, their interruptions, their directions to others cutting across the action or business on hand. This continuity may be likened to the visual continuity of the cinema. Diderot, like certain avant-garde directors of our own time, has broken away from the documentary to demonstrate the fuller possibilities of a new artistic form, better able to present realism.

Closely allied to the whole question of the interweaving of events is the use of the technique of flashbacks, common to both the cinema and the modern novel, and already to be found in Diderot's work. Its examination will help to bring out curious differences in procedure. Flashbacks disturb the usual sequence of time and events. Through the overlapping of several layers of time and event a deeper reality may often be reached. Diderot's vivid style brings his retrospection very close, and conveys the illusion of reality, which is that of the cinematographic permanent present. When used in literature, by Proust in *A la recherche du temps perdu* or by Mauriac in *Thérèse Desqueyroux*, it is the result of a process of association of ideas based on involuntary memory. Diderot, however, proceeds rather differently. Memory of the past plays its part, but the conscious mind of the protagonist is at work in the recreative process, and the author himself takes a hand in a far more jerky sequence than is to be found in a play or novel. The flash-back device is, of course, conducive to realism, since life is never lived entirely in the present, but incorporates a past and potential experience, and involves a reciprocal relationship between the individuals in society at any given moment in time. The emphasis on a lively and varied rhythm of time and event is characteristic of many avant-garde films, which endeavour to express man's inner impulses.

Miss Ann Doubell who, in an undergraduate dissertation of undoubted originality, first drew my attention to the parallel between Diderot's technique in *Jacques le Fataliste* and that to be found in the cinema, referred to *Entr'acte*, a film made by René Clair in 1924, the second part of which is a total expression of rhythmic movement, and more pertinently to the Ingmar Bergman film *Wild Strawberries* made in 1958, which is composed of a drift of loosely inter-related memories and actual happenings in the same way as *Jacques le Fataliste*. Miss Doubell also linked his technique with the 'stream of consciousness' and other techniques used by such writers as Virginia Woolf, James Joyce and Camus (in *L'Etranger*). Certainly the interplay of several dialogues, and the carrying forward of several overlapping episodes, which helped to destroy strict literary form, characterizes much contemporary writing, and with increasing frequency characters in books acquire authenticity through action and dialogue springing from the subconscious. There are important divergences, however, which are more striking. With Diderot, the conscious mind is in effective control, and the author's role remains greater. Although Diderot broke with the prevailing form of pseudo-memoirs, and moved towards objectivity in the presentation of events and characters, the whole question of author–character relationship is presented in peculiar terms, as H. Dieckmann and others have pointed out. Diderot is closer to Pirandello in whose play *Six Characters in search of an Author* the characters discuss their roles with the actors. In short, Diderot has the sophistication of modern investigations into the nature of reality and its presentation; but his answer is distinctive. It hinges on his own general philosophy and aesthetic, his way of perceiving reality, and the nature of his creative imagination. The direction of his enquiry, however, and his efforts to give authenticity to his fiction, are more intelligible today than in the eighteenth or nineteenth century, in the light of modern experiments on somewhat parallel lines. The cinema has thus led to a better understanding of Diderot's realism and of his art. If *pré-cinéma* is to have a meaning—and the *Cahiers de l'Association Internationale des Etudes Françaises*, No. 20, 'Littérature française et cinéma', for the year 1968, shows present interest in the subject—it is by enriching an objective commentary of the written text through drawing attention to curious parallels in technique. There is no intention, of course, of transforming Diderot into the forerunner of cinema technique because his last novel reads at times like a film that is being projected.

At the philosophical level, imitation of nature in Diderot's novels may be seen to have been transformed through a richer interpretation of nature, which allows scope for creative imagination. In this process memory plays a part and the images of the past are rearranged in a chosen perspective. Diderot's own imagination was largely visual; and attitude and gesture, especially combined in *tableaux*, form the basis of his increased power of dramatic communication. Without ever transcending the bounds of the real world, his imagination enabled him to broaden his conception of reality, so as to include fantasy. The incongruous, the capricious, the apparently illogical, the romantic, as well as verisimilitude in documented facts and events, severally contribute to the total truth of the complex and ever-changing reality we perceive in real life. But only great art and sophisticated techniques can heighten our powers of illusion so as to lead us to an awareness of this truth. 'Le ciel du peintre n'est pas celui de l'univers', he wrote in the *Salon* of 1767, and elsewhere: 'Eclairez vos objets selon votre soleil, qui n'est pas celui de la nature; soyez le disciple de l'arc-en-ciel, mais n'en soyez pas l'esclave'.[10] The artist must re-create his own truth, find his own images, the better to convey the totality of experience seen through his unique vision. Diderot, in his continuous search for the exact expression of the diversity and flow of life and thought, discovered the flexibility of dialectics, and within that specialized form passed from the use of static symbols to that of mobile and rhythmic sequences, better suited to the re-creation of the complexities of living.

R. NIKLAUS

REFERENCES

1 *Mimesis*, 1946, Epilogue.
2 *L'Esthétique sans paradoxe de Diderot*, 1950.
3 *Œuvres complètes de Diderot*, ed. Assézat–Tourneux, VII, p. 378.
4 A.–T., VII, p. 386.
5 *Diderot Critique d'Art et le Problème de l'Expression*, Aix-en-Provence, 1964, to be published in an amended form in *Diderot Studies*, Vol. XIII.
6 A.–T., VII, p. 385.
7 A.–T., V, p. 58.
8 A.–T., VI, p. 158.
9 A.–T., VI, p. 108.
10 A.–T., XII, p. 87.

LE BRUN-PINDARE (1729–1807)

Ponce Denis Ecouchard Le Brun, or Lebrun-Pindare as he was called, had a high opinion of himself which he managed to impose on his contemporaries, and which he expressed in one of his Odes (VI, xxiii) as follows:

> Elève du second Racine,
> Ami de l'Immortel Buffon,
> J'osai, sur la double colline
> Allier Lucrèce et Newton.
> Des badinages de Catulle
> Aux pleurs du sensible Tibulle
> On m'a vu passer tour à tour,
> Et sur les ailes de Pindare,
> Sans craindre le destin d'Icare,
> Voler jusqu'à l'Astre du Jour.

What all this means is that he thought he had excelled in didactic poetry, the elegy, and the ode.

Poetic reputations were easily made and unmade in the eighteenth century. It was enough, very often, to attract the patronage of some rich gentleman (such as the Prince de Conti and the comte de Vaudreuil in Le Brun's case—although he also lost his savings through the bankruptcy of the Prince de Guémené); or to get your name mentioned publicly by Voltaire, as he did; or to be in the encyclopaedic swim, as he was; or to obtain the suffrage of some intelligent woman (such as Madame Vigée-Lebrun, who publicly crowned our poet as Pindar, at a banquet). You could achieve fame by dying of hunger in a garret or cutting your throat, leaving behind enough for a slim volume. You could attack Fréron, Marmontel and La Harpe in turn, as he did, and deliver hundreds of epigrams at people who lacked the wit to reply. You could excel by either being elected to the Académie at an early age, or attacking it in dozens of epigrams like the following:

> Amendez-vous, ô Jetoniers gloutons;
> Faites ensemble une Œuvre expiatoire;
> A l'indigent remettez vos jetons,
> Et, s'il se peut, travaillez pour la Gloire.

Such shafts did not prevent Le Brun from joining the Académie when the time came. You could also celebrate an occasional battle, with an ode, or announce your intention to produce an enormous philosophical work in a few years' time, during which period you drew a pension and lived in one of the attics in the Louvre at the State's expense. Le Brun managed to do all of these things except cutting his throat. While he suffered from a bad moral reputation, he contrived to eke out his existence by a bluff, although he had some real talent which might have developed authentically in any other period than that. He was weak enough to allow himself to be perverted by a society in which honesty and dishonesty so often went hand in hand.

Poetic reputations had to be made to some extent in spite of the prevailing outlook. The emphasis in prose was laid on the vulgarization of philosophical and scientific thought, or in creative literature on the novel and the theatre; yet everyone thought it would be disgraceful if this failed to be a great age for poetry. So they had Jean-Baptiste Rousseau, Louis Racine, Voltaire, and Le Brun. It also became almost inevitable that, socially, the most successful poetry would be either in *vers de société*, or that which reflected the philosophical movement. Such events as the Lisbon disaster allowed dozens of poets to theorize about Nature and manifest some Sensibility at the same time. Such events, treated hot, earned you the title *Pindare* after your name. Fame could also be got by writing essays in verse, after the manner of Pope. Although lip-service was paid to Sensibility, the breakdown of the French pastoral tradition since La Fontaine resulted in thin gruel, filtered through J.-B. Rousseau, while the purely descriptive verse of the age lacked originality and was generally a facile reproduction of foreign models. In a period of scientific exploration the poets seemed incapable of *seeing* the world around them as it really was, except through a fog of mythology and archaic diction which blunted the imagination.

If the English poets of the eighteenth century managed to get themselves called Augustans (by Goldsmith in 1759), this was not the case in France, where although the ethos was very much the same, the gravity of thought and the mature poise and tone of a Pope or Johnson were not often achieved. Maybe the reason for this was that the English had already established a Roundhead poetry, as opposed to the decadent academic and aristocratic French tradition.

None the less, to his contemporaries—and a long life enables a poet to impose himself on more than one generation, so that a Le Brun could draw pensions from Louis XV, Louis XVI and finally Bonaparte—'Pindar' had the outward appearance, *faute de mieux*, of being a great Augustan. He admired all the right people, such as Horace and Tibullus, Pindar, Voltaire, and himself. In loudly proclaiming his apprenticeship to Louis Racine (whose doomed son was his close friend), Le Brun hitched himself on to the great Classical tradition, or rather the legend of it. He strengthened this claim by winning the limelight in 1760 through persuading Voltaire, by means of a widely publicized ode, to succour the nephew and the great-niece of Corneille. Then, as 'l'ami de l'immortel Buffon' to whom he offered many poems and with whom he maintained an obsequious correspondence, he appeared likely to dominate the stream of didactic poetry which in fact found a better though still imperfect expression in Voltaire, Saint-Lambert, Delille, Chénier, and even 'le malheureux Roucher'. Le Brun lived for nearly fifty years on the promise of a vast work, *La Nature*, which was to be a poetical rendering of Buffon's thought. But we look in vain for the child of Lucretius and Newton in this opus, which never appeared in his lifetime.

When it came to be published at last, by Ginguené, in the collected works of Le Brun in four volumes in 1811, the editor gave its title as follows: *La Nature, ou le Bonheur Philosophique et Champêtre, Poème en Quatre Chants*. This does not correspond exactly with Le Brun's announcement of a vast philosophical and scientific work. Further, the editor had to comment, 'Commencé en 1760, et dont à l'exception du Troisième Chant, qui est presque entier, il n'existe que des fragments'.

It is not our intention to 'appreciate' this unfinished ruin. Although Le Brun wrote in a preface to one of his odes in 1762, 'L'objet le plus sublime de la Poésie, c'est d'être utile', there is nothing very useful to anybody in *La Nature*, and the quotable passages are not often interesting for the reasons that he intended. Like his contemporaries, including Delille and Chénier himself, Le Brun had not found—and perhaps no poet has ever found—a satisfactory manner of presenting scientific thought in verse. This is how Le Brun wrote about the human voice:

> O Voix, Fille de l'Air, dis-nous quelle est ta route?
> Dis comment du Larinx vers la Glotte élancé,
> A l'aide du Palais ma langue a prononcé
> Le son qui sur ma lèvre impatiente d'éclore,
> Divise ses rayons, forme un Cône sonore,
> Air lui-même, remplit l'Air de mes Accens,
> Franchit la Pesanteur, roule au-dessus des Vents,
> De Globule en Globule, rapide Merveille,
> Attache ma pensée aux fibres de l'Oreille.

Such foolish lines destroy Le Brun's claim to be a great didactic poet. Even if the rest of the work were satisfactory, which it is not, they would be an unpardonable blemish.

Apart from this unfulfilled promise, which may be forgiven in view of the fate of most works of that kind, Le Brun rendered to poetry one or two services which were not unimportant. His *Discours sur Tibulle* (1763) helped to widen the scope of the elegy, as we shall see later. Maybe his many attacks on contemporary poetry prevented it from being even worse than it became, and he handed on this message of energy and virility to André Chénier, as well as strengthening and perhaps guiding his classical studies. Many of Chénier's ideas are to be found, though not so well expressed, in Le Brun, for instance in *Odes*, I, xxv (*Que l'Etude de la Nature est préférable même à celle des Anciens*:

> Soyez donc, Ombres immortelles,
> Mes Guides, et non pas mes Modelles;
> Qu'un autre rampe à vos genoux;
> Il est une gloire plus sûre:
> Vous n'imitiez que la Nature,
> Et je l'imite comme vous—

or

FRANCIS SCARFE

> La Nature fait les Homères,
> L'Art fait les poètes vulgaires.

His ode on Enthusiasm (II, i) does not appear to have been published before 1792, but Chénier probably had some anterior knowledge of it: in spite of this poem's reputation there is little to be saved from it, now that we have got over the romantic notion of inspiration. The ode *Sur le faux goût des poésies modernes* (V, xii) is typical of him in another way, with its combination of elegance and malice:

> Ce n'est pas sous de verds treillages
> Où l'Art sut courber les feuillages,
> Qu'un Rossignol charme les Airs;
> Ses mélodieuses veillées,
> Sous les Forêts échevelées,
> Prodiguent leurs plus doux Concerts.

> Ni l'Art, ni sa riche imposture,
> Rien ne répare la Nature
> Qui manque aux rimes de Bernis;
> D'Azur il peint une Cabane;
> Et son Art, au pinceau d'Albane,
> Prête d'infidèles Vernis . . ..

> La Nature a de vrais Prodiges;
> Et rejetant les vains Prestiges,
> Les monstrueux Enchantemens,
> Laisse à Pékin encor barbare,
> Renverser, d'un crayon bizarre,
> L'ordre antique des Élémens.

Le Brun left six books of odes, amounting to some 142 pieces. The *Ode sur la Ruine de Lisbonne* (I, ix) was published in 1756 and brought him early fame although a large number of odes (and even 'comic' poems) were written on the subject. His success might be to some extent attributed to the fact that this publication was accompanied by a brilliantly-written essay, 'Réflexions sur le Génie de l'Ode' which showed that he knew what he was talking about. In attacking La Motte ('homme à définitions s'il en fut jamais') he ranged himself, even at this late date, on the side of the 'Anciens', but the way in which he did so presaged well for the future, had he been listened to or had he listened to himself.

Aucun genre de poésie n'échappe plus [que l'Ode] au compas géométrique; aucun n'est plus exposé à ces caprices heureux que l'art ne saurait prévoir, à ces fougues du génie, qui souvent arrive à son but sans trop connaître lui-même les sentiers qu'il a pris.

Le Brun had the makings of a good critic, but he wasted this gift through spiteful jealousies. Apart from his attacks on contemporary poets he had moments of enormous insight, such as 'Bossuet pouvait être Pindare: il en respire le caractère; que de sublimes morceaux dans ses panégyriques n'attendent que les vers pour être des odes admirables'. This tribute from an atheist is as unexpected as Paul Valéry's. There is also a very fine passage on Montesquieu, ending 'Ce qu'il y a de singulier, c'est qu'aimant l'Ode assez médiocrement, il ait donné à sa prose le ton dithyrambique'. Pindar, Horace, Anacreon, Ronsard, he wrote of in lyrical terms, but (like Chénier, whom he perhaps influenced in this respect) he had certain reservations about Malherbe: although he admired the La Rochelle ode, he wrote 'Si l'Art peut suppléer à la Nature, il fut poète; la sécheresse de son génie perce quelquefois à travers ses cadences heureuses et le tour harmonieux de ses vers'.

Le Brun's ode on the Lisbon catastrophe is of fairly consistent quality and shows him to be already a master of the strophe, as well as having a certain energy or vitality which stands out against the slackness of much verse of that period. To take only a small sample (the second stanza):

> Mortel superbe! folle Argile,
> Cherche tes destins éclipsés:
> De la Terre habitant fragile
> Tes pas à peine y sont tracés.
> Quoi! son berceau touche à la tombe?

Échappé du Néant, il tombe
Dans le noir oubli du cercueil:
Ses jours sont des éclairs rapides
Qu'engloutissent des Nuits avides:
Quel espace pour tant d'orgueil!

The biblical tone is well grasped, but it has some typical weaknesses.
The first is the rhyme of the homonyms *tombe . . . tombe*. The second
is what might be considered as an unsuccessful shift from the second
to the third person (tes pas . . . son berceau) which was unnecessary.
Le Brun's obsession with form usually made for good structure and
metre, but sometimes at the expense of logic. He was often just in
sight of perfection, but only reached it in one poem, the ode on
Le Vengeur to which we shall return later.

It was natural that this gift of energy should be accompanied by
a certain moral courage, which comes out in the *Ode à M. de Buffon
sur ses détracteurs*, and another early success, *A M. de Voltaire, en
faveur de Mlle Corneille* (I, xxiv). He wrote the latter ode in 1760,
and as a result of it Voltaire took the girl to Ferney and adopted her.
Le Brun had the characteristically bad taste to print, in Geneva,
Voltaire's letters on the subject, together with his poem which
Voltaire so sincerely admired that he forgave the young poet. To
take, again, only a sample, this is how he represents the great
Corneille addressing his descendant:

Si le nom de Corneille est ton seul héritage,
Cette Gloire n'est point un stérile partage:
O ma Fille! ta dot est l'Immortalité;
Et je laisse à ton sort, que mon Destin protège,
    Mes Lauriers pour cortège:
Leur Ombre sert d'asile à ma Postérité.

Comme un jeune Palmier, levant sa noble tête,
Sous l'ombre paternelle affronte la tempête,
Rival du Cèdre altier qui règne sur les Monts;
Si ton Nom fut le mien, et si mon Sang t'anime,
    Lève un front magnanime;
Ma Race peut marcher rivale des Bourbons.

This has, again, certain weaknesses (laurels can hardly form a cortege), but if in some ways it prefigures the 'emphase' of the early Hugo, it is energetic and the second of the above stanzas has something of the genuine Augustan tone.

However, in all these odes it is hard to find one without some fault, except perhaps some pleasant but trivial drinking-songs in the manner of Horace and others. Sainte-Beuve was perhaps right in saying 'Le talent lyrique de Le Brun est grand, quelquefois immense, presque partout incomplet' (*Portraits Littéraires*, Pléiade, *Oeuvres*, *I*, p. 790) but even then, in that essay he exaggerated Le Brun's qualities because of his association with André Chénier, and perhaps, also, as Faguet suggested, because he saw some connection between Le Brun and Hugo. Sainte-Beuve thought that Le Brun found 'images sublimes' whenever writing about such things as genius or enthusiasm; but he seems to me to be at his best, and worst, when he is attacking something: as the remarkable *Epigrammes* show, he had primarily a satirical and even destructive talent. Examples of this in the odes are to be found in II, xxv, *Sur l'Etat de Décadence de la Monarchie Française durant la Dernière Moitié du Règne de Louis XV* (he liked such long titles), or IV, i, *Aux Français* with its prophetic note:

> Français, ressaisissez le Char de la Victoire;
> Aux Armes, Citoyens! il faut tenter le Sort.
> Il n'est que deux Sentiers dans les Champs de la Gloire:
> Le Triomphe ou la Mort,

or in IV, xi, *Sur l'Ennui*, or V, x, *Contre le Luxe* in which he finds some 'noble accents' in condemning slavery: here is Nature speaking:

> Où prétendent voler ces Forêts vagabondes?
> La Patrie à vos yeux est-elle sans appas?
> Pourquoi fatiguez-vous les deux Mers, les deux Mondes?
> Le Bonheur germait sous vos pas.
>
> Le Niger a vendu ses Fils et son Rivage
> A vos Brigands d'Europe! et, si nous les croyons,
> Flambeau sacré du Jour, cet indigne esclavage
> Est le Crime de tes Rayons!

Here the image of ships as 'forêts vagabondes' is brilliant, although it is isolated; the overall movement is compelling.

Sainte-Beuve had some good fun with the passage 'Vanvres, qu'habite Galathée' in V, i, *Le Triomphe de nos Paysages*, but that ode is one of Le Brun's most agreeable, paradoxically showing how an excess of linguistic sophistication results, in the end (as was often the case with the so-called Baroque poets), in an effect of naïveness. In English critical terms, Le Brun's drift was more towards Fancy than towards Imagination, and that goes for most of the work of his contemporaries. Another ode which I would preserve for the same rather uncritical reason, that it has a period charm and also proves the fallacy of removing poetry too far from common speech, is VI, ii, the delightful *Mes Souvenirs, ou les Deux Rives de la Seine*. This is how he described such childhood games as whipping tops, skipping, shuttlecock and kite-flying:

> Là, dans sa vitesse immobile,
> Le buis semblait dormir, agité par mes bras;
> Là, je triplais le cercle agile
> Du chanvre envolé sur mes pas.
>
> Là, frêle émule de Dédale,
> Un liége, sous mes coups, se plut à voltiger;
> Là, dans une course rivale
> J'étais Achille au pas léger.
>
> Là, j'élevais jusqu'à la nue
> Ce long fantôme ailé, qu'un fil dirige encor,
> A travers la route inconnue
> Qu'Eole ouvre à son vague essor.

All that was a disease of language, no doubt, and if here it seems appropriate enough, it explains why the more serious odes have not held their place in the tradition, with the exception of the one which is now his only claim to celebrity, *Sur le Vaisseau LE VENGEUR* (V, xxiii). In this ode, for once, Le Brun's mannerisms, his overload of classical allusions, the circumlocutions and inflated tone, find some justification. It is as if his laborious apprenticeship to the ode was intended for this celebration of one genuine though minor heroic event: the *Vengeur* sinking with its crew rather than capitulate to the English.

It is typical of Le Brun's vanity, that out of seventeen stanzas, half of them are devoted to himself. But the first eight are not unworthy of him or indeed of any poet, with such lines as

> Vainqueur d'Eole et des Pléiades,
> Je sens d'un souffle heureux mon Navire emporté:
> Il échappe aux écueils des trompeuses Cyclades,
>   Il vogue à l'Immortalité.
>
> Mais des Flots fût-il la Victime,
> Ainsi que le VENGEUR il est beau de périr;
> Il est beau, quand le Sort vous plonge dans l'Abîme,
>   De paraître le conquérir.

The second of the above stanzas is the ninth, or central one, of the seventeen. The structure of the poem is thus perfect in its conception, in which the poet's self-glorification (accompanied by some doubt) and the doomed ship come together, in a way that might have influenced Rimbaud's *Bateau Ivre*. This central quatrain thus serves as a hinge on which the two parts of the poem turn, while at the same time announcing the theme of triumph in disaster which is restated in the poem's concluding lines, as follows:

> Et vous! Héros de Salamine,
> Dont Thétis vante encor les exploits glorieux,
> Non! vous n'égalez point cette auguste Ruine,
>   Ce Naufrage victorieux!

This is perhaps the only poem by Le Brun which shows any real act of imagination, and it is one of the finest pieces of *poésie de circonstance* in the French language.

Le Brun managed to establish himself as a public poet, but there is a certain test in what a writer makes of his own immediate experience, which is not unimportant when considering a period which claimed to be an age of Sensibility as well as of Reason. In him we find a seriously limited and even maimed sensibility: but was it entirely his fault, or the result of an inhibition common to the age? Before Chénier and Parny we do not often find a satisfying formulation of feeling. Even in Chénier's elegies the shades of Tibullus, Horace and many another hover in the background and overshadow the heart. We can never be sure whether the poets were writing what they wanted to, or whether it was what they thought they ought to write. Le Brun occasionally revealed the depths, in his elegies; but they were the depths, rather, of negative feeling.

One of his most useful contributions was to draw attention to Tibullus. This he did with a few versions of his own and his influential *Discours sur Tibulle* in 1763. His drawing of attention away from Ovid and Propertius amounted to a revision of taste—one which was to have consequences for Chénier, Thomas, and Parny (whom Voltaire addressed as 'mon petit Tibulle'). Le Brun reproached Ovid for having 'plus d'esprit que de sentiment, plus de coquetterie que de tendresse': whether this is true or not, the *Amores* and *Ars Amatoria* had a consistently bad influence in France, for Ovid's elegant cynicism was no longer offset by the refining influence of Petrarch or the Provençal poets for almost two centuries. Le Brun said that Propertius 'soupire savamment', while Catullus elegantly treated 'des sujets légers et badins'. At the same time he condemned a number of elegiac poets of his own time, 'cette foule moderne d'auteurs gentils, d'écrivains en pastel, et de poètes vernisseurs', it being his habit to elbow everyone else out of his way. Unlike his contemporaries he also condemned English influences.

One of Le Brun's constant themes was that of the superiority of rural over city life, but as with most writers of the period he never came close to a real experience in those terms. When he tried to, it was usually wrapped in conventional diction or spoiled by some facetious incongruity, as in the following:

> Heureux qui de Palès respirant tous les charmes,
> Va surprendre l'Aurore à ses premières larmes,

Et d'un pied matineux effleurant le gazon,
De l'Oiseau qui s'éveille entend le premier son!
Heureux, si le premier cueillant la fleur naissante,
J'en pare ton beau sein, ô ma fidèle Amante!
Ou d'un nid que la feuille à peine couvre encor,
Je mets sur tes genoux le frêle et doux trésor;
Et la timide Mère, inquiète, éperdue,
Qui le protège encor de son aile étendue!
Mais, j'entends les regrets du Père et de l'Epoux!
O ma Fanni, cédons à des regrets si doux.
Ah! remettons ce nid dans son palais mobile;
Croissez, petits Oiseaux! goûtez un sort tranquille;
Que jamais l'épervier, ni l'Autour ravisseur,
Ni le plomb criminel lancé par le Chasseur,
N'abrègent de vos jours l'innocente durée,
Et ne fassent gémir une Veuve éplorée.

I have not seen this Watteauesque theme of the bird's nest treated
elsewhere, and must give credit to Le Brun for some originality, but
it is one which invites and gets a nauseatingly sentimental treatment.
There is a softness of tone of which La Fontaine would not have
been guilty, and which reduces the *Père* . . . *époux* . . . *veuve* to
frivolity. The reader, in trying to take all this, is forced to induce a
special state of mind comparable with that which is necessary, at
this date, to read some of the Romantics, even though it is quite
possible that Le Brun started from a personal experience. It might
have been lived, but the expression is hopelessly blurred: eighteenth-
century Sensibility had to draw attention to itself, as he does here—
now I am being tender, now I am being sensitive, look, I'm a nature-
lover. All this amounts to what Baudelaire condemned as 'la manie
de tout dire'.

In many respects, and especially in the novel, many of Le
Brun's contemporaries showed a robust enough attitude to love,
distinguishing little between the sentiment and its erotic manifestations. Maybe the two ought logically to go together, as in the
Elizabethans and Donne, but in eighteenth-century France eroticism

usually split into polite insincerity on the one hand and coarse vulgarity on the other. Not that we look for excessive refinements, but Le Brun will begin a so-called elegy with a loud cockerel note, as in

> O Nuit voluptueuse! O Lit cent fois heureux!
> Asile et Confident des Baisers amoureux,
> Lit, où j'ai caressé mon Amante fidelle;
> Rideaux que le Plaisir agitait autour d'elle.
>
> (Élég. II, iv)

An even more comic grossness is to be found in one of the *Odes* (IV, xx):

> Heureux Coussin, dont la Plume repousse
> La Volupté, pour servir ses ébats;
> Ah! garde bien une empreinte si douce!
> Mol édredon, ne te relève pas!

With all their familiar touches, Le Brun's amorous verses were less blunt and matter-of-fact than those of Donne or Marvell, where a frank eroticism is usually a point of departure for some serious judgement on existence. Good taste is not just a matter of barring certain themes or holds: in the case of Le Brun's elegies the fundamental error is one of human focus, woman being little more than a love-object or a doll:

> Sans doute un demi-jour sert mieux la Volupté,
> Et j'aime à voir rougir la timide Beauté.

The problem of how to get this aspect of experience into poetry was not solved before Parny and Chénier, where the metaphysical dimension was also frequently lacking. Le Brun himself was conscious of the possibility of some greater depth and refinement, and wrote (I, vii)

> Des vulgaires Amans la paisible tendresse
> Jamais n'a pu sentir, calme dans son ivresse,
> D'un cœur passionné les troubles orageux.
> S'ils connaissent l'Amour, ce n'est que par ses jeux.

O Sensibilité, présent cher et funeste!
Que d'amertume, hélas, dans ton Nectar céleste!
Toujours de son bonheur un cœur tendre est puni!

But it is not in writing *about* Sensibility, that sensibility manifests itself: it should inform the whole work, as it does in Chénier. This is not to say that Le Brun's elegies can no longer be read at all; but if they are to be read it can only be for good isolated lines, or for a demonstration of the faults of his period, which in him are concentrated.

What Le Brun brought into the Elegy was something incompatible with the elegiac tone: that is to say, anger and hatred. This occurred as a result of his divorce, when his wife, mother and sister turned against him and seized all his belongings. The proceedings went on for seven years and did him no credit, though the fact that he was to know poverty, disgrace and blindness compensates to some extent. This dried up any elegiac talent he might have had: he could write such repulsive 'elegies' as *A Némésis*, cursing his whole family:

Que de fois, Némésis, dans ce funeste Orage,
Mon fragile Vaisseau fut voisin du Naufrage....
Tu vis le triple nœud de ce Complot infâme;
Tu vis s'armer ensemble et Mère, et Sœur, et Femme;
Tu vis leur noire Audace, ô Crime! ô triple horreur!
De leurs coups sur moi seul diriger la fureur....

He reached the summit of bad taste in all the elegies against his own family, but overpassed it in II, iii in which he invited his unborn child to loathe its mother, in overtones which reflect Horace's Epode against Canidia. It would be a relief to find in the elegies on his son's death some genuine sign of tenderness or remorse, but in II, vii, such Malherbian lines as

Muses! donnez des Fleurs à sa tombe légère:
Toi, Vénus! dont le Myrte honora son berceau,
Hélas, d'un noir Cyprès couronne son tombeau.
Tu n'es plus, ô mon Fils! trop semblable à la rose,

E

Sous tes pas innocens nouvellement éclose,
La Parque a moissonné tes rapides instans,
Lorsqu'à peine tes yeux ont revu le Printemps :
Né dans le mois des Fleurs, tu disparais comme elles—

are followed by such venomous outbursts as

> Ah ! tu l'avais frappé de tes Vœux homicides,
> Mère affreuse ! ta Haine et la Mort, tour à tour,
> M'enlèvent une Amante et les fruits de l'Amour.

The third Book with its adaptations of Tibullus is perhaps the best, but in the seventh elegy of that series Le Brun is found addressing himself to a fifteen-year-old girl in a convent, whom he seduced: the commonplaces of eighteenth-century fiction were not excluded from life as it was then lived, and Le Brun found no new manner of expressing them.

There is not much point in looking longer at Le Brun's elegies. Of the conclusions that may be drawn, the first is that Le Brun was one of those responsible for the breakdown of the *genre* which was to be further continued by the Romantics: the faults of tone, the falsifying of feeling, the violence and negative emotions show a fundamental uncertainty which, in Le Brun's case, came largely from the fact that he never really believed that poetry should be personal, but that the poet should 'sing' such great subjects as war, glory, and liberty. The second conclusion is that Le Brun wrote his elegies only for immediate profit—the conquest of some woman, or his own self-justification: in other words he reduced the elegy to a form of *poésie de circonstance*.

That Le Brun did not take the elegy seriously and perhaps failed in it for that reason, comes out very well in his *Epîtres*, which together with the *Epigrammes* contain some of his best writing. The *Epître* is one of the most interesting of eighteenth-century *genres*, from Voltaire right down to André Chénier. In it the tone can be informal and relaxed, in fact all tones and mixtures of tones and all types of themes and forms are possible in it. Much of the best poetry of the

century, which was a social period *par excellence*, got into the Epistle,
for it could serve both public and private ends, and range from a
recipe for soup, as in Voltaire, to the treatment of serious philosophical matters, or, as in Le Brun's excellent *Sur la Bonne et
Mauvaise Plaisanterie*, to acute satire. If Le Brun's satirical Epistles
are on the whole the best, an exception is the famous one addressed
to André Chénier ('Oui, l'astre du Génie éclaira ton berceau', I, ii)
and a number of others with a genial and familiar tone.

But what interests me at the moment is the humorous way in
which, in his epistles, Le Brun demolished his own elegies. The
epistle I, iv has the sub-title 'Que les Vers sont plus nuisibles
qu'utiles en Amour'. Apart from isolated sparkling lines, he develops
the theme with an elegance that would have done honour to
Voltaire:

> Le Dieu des Vers, tu le sais, ma Thémire,
> 　　　Est le Dieu qui répand le Jour.
> Cent fois il a trahi les mystères d'Amour.
> Les Vers sont indiscrets: ils aiment à paraître.
> Un secret mis en vers cesse bientôt de l'être.
> Mais tu dis que son Art rend l'Amour plus charmant;
> Vante moins de cet art le frivole agrément.
> L'âme ne s'écrit point: les rimes cadencées
> Voilent d'un faux éclat ses naïves pensées.
> 　　　Orner l'Amour, c'est le trahir;
> Lui-même est sa parure: on ne peut l'embellir.
> La candeur n'est qu'un fard du moment qu'elle est peinte:
> L'âme perd de ses feux, même en les exprimant:
> 　　　L'Amour s'évapore en rimant.
> L'esprit n'est point sans Art, et nul Art n'est sans feinte.

Such debunking is worth all his elegies put together. He took up
the same theme, but in the opposite sense, in II, ix, *Que la vraie
poésie est favorable à l'Amour*, and this time managed to mock some
of his contemporary poets and decide

> Ah, sans doute en amour les Vers sont impuissants,
> Ils sont plus dangereux qu'utiles

> Quand l'Esprit, aux flâmes subtiles,
> Les compose de fard, de vernis, et d'encens . . .

Le Brun went further, by taking some of the stock themes of the elegy and handling them lightly and humorously in the epistles: for instance in II, vii, the story of a missed appointment in which he poked fun at the traditional serenade, or perhaps *aubade*:

> Vous m'eussiez vu, plus tendre, et plus touchant encore,
> Sous le voile peu sûr d'un léger Parasol
> Que battait l'orageuse pluie,
> Charmer de votre nom ma Guitare attendrie,
> Plus langoureux qu'un Espagnol
> Chantant la Beauté qu'il ennuie.

Such lines take us back to the 'badinage' of Desportes. In the same piece he also makes fun of the lover's dream:

> Hélas, quand je perdais raison, temps, vers et prose,
> Mouillé, transi, plaintif et rebuté,
> Sans doute un Songe heureux vous couronnait de Rose;
> Je goûtais l'Amertume, et vous la Volupté.
> Peut-être même alors, sous un voile complice,
> D'un œil malin et curieux
> Vous jouissiez de mon supplice,
> Et riant . . . non, ce doute est trop injurieux!
> Non, vos yeux n'eurent point cette noire malice:
> Ils sont trop beaux pour être si cruels;
> Ils sont indifférents, et non pas criminels.

The existence of such lines is a useful corrective to our usual view of the eighteenth century, but they also pinpoint the insecurity of the poet's self-important stance. Few of Le Brun's letters have survived—from what must have been an enormous correspondence—but they sometimes show him to have been a more attractive character than legend would have it. He wrote to the comte de Brancas, from the country (T. IV, *Lettre* LXI):

Je vous prie de croire, M. le Comte, que si je n'étais pas mort ici d'une fluxion de poitrine, assurément je vous aurais donné plutôt de mes nouvelles. Si vous trouvez cette excuse assez bonne, vous me permettrez de vous donner la recette aussi prompte que charmante d'une mort tout-à-fait pastorale. Dansez, comme j'ai fait, depuis sept heures du soir jusqu'à neuf, sur un tapis de gazon plus brillant et plus verd que l'émeraude; respirez, en dansant, la délicieuse fraîcheur des bois et des prairies, tandis que la douce rosée s'élève et retombe sur la terre en perles liquides, et vous éprouverez comme moi que ce qui ferait en vers la plus jolie existence du monde, vous donne en prose un rhume abominable.

This delightful prose brings out the common weaknesses of eighteenth-century poets in a way that perhaps a more serious demonstration could not do: the tendency to think that in order to write poetry you have to take up your lyre and put on your best wig before blotting a line; to think that experience is different according to whether it is expressed in verse or in prose; to think that Nature has to be gilded instead of being shown more or less as it is; and to think that striking definitions of poetry or genius or enthusiasm, or a refined vocabulary, will work miracles. The eighteenth century was fertile in poetic theory and theories which, on inspection, prove to have little or no relationship to the poetry that was actually written. A wrong conception of poetry *in practice*, a conventional insincerity added to his own, practically destroyed what poetic gifts Le Brun ever possessed. It cannot be said that he was not a poet, any more than that can be said about Voltaire: but his work is not much more than that of a man who knew all the accepted tricks of a trade, and who never got beyond the surface of life as a poet is expected to do, and who always chose to wear stilts. In all this he resembled Southey, and he would have made a suitable poet laureate. With all his wit and sophistication he would have been capable, like Southey, of getting a carbuncle on his head through wearing a crown of laurels. In eighteenth-century Paris, many a carbuncle blushed unseen.

FRANCIS SCARFE

'NOTTES EGALES ET INEGALES'

Quantz[1] in his famous book on how to play the transverse flute, writing about groups of crotchets, quavers, and semiquavers says that the first of every pair must be emphasized more than the second, and in short although they appear in the music as even, they should be played unevenly, thus making the first note of every pair slightly longer than the second. But he points out that this applies only to pieces that are slow to moderate in tempo, and not to very fast pieces, as there would not be time to make uneven very rapid quavers or semiquavers. Quantz only repeated what seems to have been the custom in France for a century or so, but the question has for a long time remained unanswered whether this dotting of evenly written notes was common in other countries besides France.

Many of the late seventeenth-century French theorists, and those of the eighteenth, explain about even and uneven notes in their books, and also composers write at the beginning of their pieces whether notes are 'égales' or 'inégales'.

In other countries with some exceptions the practice of altering values of notes in this way was mostly alluded to vaguely, that is in Germany and England, but it seemed that in Italy it was only once or twice mentioned. Whether or not the theorists, the composers, and the players were practising what they preached, it certainly bears out in practice that pieces of music that suggest this treatment, when played without regard to the changing of note values from that written in the music, tend to sound dull and lifeless.

Example I

Whereas in François Couperin le Grand's books of *Ordres* or *Suites*[2] there is a table of ornaments which explains that Example I is to be played so that the second note is longer than the first, thus making the first short, the effect being Example I[a],

Example I[a]

there is no corresponding direction as to when one should play Example II like Example III or Example IV.

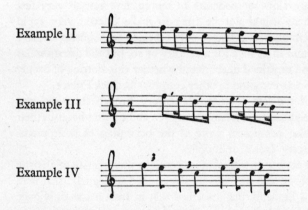

In two pieces in the fifth 'ordre', *La Badine* and *Les Vendangeuses*, there are many passages like that of Example I, but Couperin does not tell the player when he should make evenly written quavers into uneven,

If one disregards the contrasts

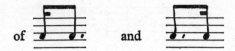

of   and

in playing the piece, the result is uninteresting. One's guide can therefore only be good musical taste. Couperin himself took pains to point out in his famous *L'Art de toucher le clavecin*[3] 'that we write differently from what we play: that is to say foreigners play our music less well than we play theirs. On the contrary the Italians write their musical notes exactly as they mean them to be heard. For example, we dot several quavers following one another conjointly although we write them equal; our custom serves us well, and we continue thus'.

If the player had only to rely on this book for advice when he should play notes uneven that are written even, it would be very difficult, but so many other writers deal with the subject in more detail than Couperin. Hotteterre in his *Treatise on the Transverse Flute*,[4] says:

one should observe well that quavers should not always be played equal, and that in certain measures one should make one long and one short; that is determined by the number of notes. If it is an even number then the first is to be made long, and the second short, and in the same way with the others. If the number is uneven one should do the opposite; that is called 'dotting'. The measures in which this is done are mostly those in two time, those in simple three time and those having six crotchets in a bar as their time signature.

Lambert[5] says much the same thing, and there were many others who wrote also about the subject in the same way.

Composers even signified when the player should play equal or unequal notes. Marin Marais, in his second book of pieces for viols and harpsichord,[6] at the twelfth 'couplet' (variation) of the

Folies d'Espagne writes this:

'signifying that it is necessary to make each note equal instead of dotting them as one usually does, the first to the second'. Marais had to write this, so he said, as most French players would make the first note of the second and third beats in this bar dotted.

Other composers, French composers, use the same dots, which came to mean staccato, to signify that the notes are equal, for only with difficulty can one make staccato notes dotted. Composers of such stature as Mondonville, Quentin and Leclair all used this sign to mean even notes. Rameau expressly wishes the player in *Les Niais de Sologne*[7] to make the quavers equal, putting the words 'Nottes égales' at the beginning of the piece.

De Caix d'Hervelois[8] in his first and second volumes of pieces for viols, marks movements with directions such as 'nottes égales', 'marqué' etc. and in his second volume,[9] *Gavotte Vaudeville-Fantaisie*, 'pointé' (dotted). Here the notes are evenly written. In fact French composers of the seventeenth and eighteenth centuries were anxious to let their interpreters know when notes were to be played equal, supposing that normally the music would have a dotted character.

It is only when music of other nations is considered, that the difficulty of interpretation arises, although so often in suites of dances it is easier to decide when it is necessary to play even or uneven notes. In the case of Purcell, and music in England in the middle to late seventeenth century which was influenced by French procedure, Sarabands and Courantes if they are French and not Italian Courantes, seem to play better if many of the notes are played uneven. The conclusion is uncertain in the case of seventeenth-century German music, and later J. S. Bach. Certainly it is impossible to say definitely that uneven notes were not used. Composers such as Froberger were much influenced by French music.

Bach's French suites for harpsichord naturally should be played in the French style, but the question whether this style should be extended to all his other works is still not solved. His knowledge of French music was profound, and in his Concertos, and large scale music, uneven playing of notes can be effective in slow movements, but the style of German music is different from that of the French. The former had its roots in the Christian religion, and organ music played a large part in its development. As Quantz had written about this subject, he must have known how music was played in Germany, but by his time French ideas and influence had completely permeated the German court circles, and presumably he was writing about his own times. Handel was different from Bach in this respect, as he was influenced by Italian music, though also by French and, later, by English. So often he only sketched out the framework of a piece, and the player had to use his ingenuity with ornaments, cadenzas, and also uneven notes when required.

The modern player may have developed by deduction and musicianship an instinct about how to perform early music, and it may seem right to him and many others, but nobody has survived these centuries to instruct us what really to do and what not to do. But one thing we do know from a composer so recent as Mozart is that players and even composers did not play other people's works or their own works as they were printed. Robert Donington[10] has done a good deal of valuable research on this matter, but there are still many more early references that may throw more light on the subject.

CHRISTOPHER WOOD

REFERENCES

1 J. J. Quantz, *Versuch einer Anweisung die Flöte traversiere zu spielen*, Berlin, 1752.
2 F. Couperin le Grand, *Ordres*, 4 volumes, Paris (1713–1730).
3 Paris, 1717.
4 Hotteterre le Romain, *Principes de la flûte traversière*, Paris, 1707.
5 M. de Saint-Lambert, *Les Principes du clavecin*, Paris, 1702.
6 *Pièces de violes*, Paris, 1692.
7 *Pièces de Clavecin*, Paris, 1731.
8 *Quatre Suites*, Paris, 1731.
9 P. 28.
10 'Communications' in *Journal of the American Musicological Society*, 1966.

LIST OF SUBSCRIBERS

Ian W. Alexander
G. W. Allan
L. Allen
Bruce Allsopp
A. C. Andison
Jessie Anwell
Jonathan R. Armitage
E. R. Ashe
L. J. Austin

E. L. Bagnall
W. A. Barber
Carl P. Barbier
H. T. Barnwell
Jennifer J. Beard
E. Beaumont
B. W. Beckingsale
Jocelyn E. Beeley
Sr. Bénédicte Marie
D. G. Berry
T. Besterman
C. J. Betts
A. Birney
R. F. Bisson
Margaret Blake
Prudence Bliss
Constance Braithwaite
K. W. Britton
W. S. Brooks
A. W. Brown
Stephanie Brown
J. H. Brumfitt,
Dr. & Mrs. H. O. Bull
C. A. Burns
A. Burstall

Joseph A. Chapman
D. R. Chevallier
G. J. Cheyne
J. Christie
Joyce Christie
John G. Clark
F. W. Clayton
H. P. Clive
J. M. Cocking
N. Cohn
B. B. Connolly
C. P. Courtney
Sr. Gillian Craig
Paul Crowther

Norman & Margaret Cullen

Joy Ann Davidson
Josephine Davies
M. Gerard Davis
Doris Delacourcelle
Edith F. Devlin
Marilyn Disney
Mary E. Dodds
Winifred Donkin
Elfrieda Dubois
C. R. Duckworth
Marjorie E. Duff
C. J. Duncan
R. Dunn

Thelma Edwards
C. Ellenby
R. S. Elmes
Joan S. Emmerson

A. W. Fairbairn
Alison Fairlie
J. S. Falconer
J. F. Falvey
Peter R. Fawcett
Liliane Fearn
R. S. Firth
Brian T. Fitch
G. B. A. Fletcher
J. Foster
J. H. Fox
R. A. Francis
Constance M. Frazer
Eric A. Freedman
P. A. Fryer
N. A. Furness

J. H. Gawler
Austin Gill
C. M. Girdlestone
Joan Gladstone
K. O. Gore
D. W. S. Gray
Gordon Green
J. Duchesne-Guillemin

Brian Hackett
C. A. Hackett
H. Gaston Hall

G. E. M. Hallett
Norman Hampson
J. Hampton
M. G. Harris
I. Hindmarsh
Alan Hodge
R. B. Holland
T. E. Hope
W. D. Howarth

W. N. Ince
G. W. Ireland
Peter G. Isaac

Eva Jacobs
S. John
A. H. Johnson
C. Johnston
O. R. Johnston
Rhys S. Jones
Rudolf Jud
Mary Judge

P. Kelly
Joanna Kitchin

S. J. Larkin
F. W. Leakey
R. A. Leigh
J. N. Lindop
J. Lough
R. W. Lovel
J. Lovell

J. R. McDiarmid
James McFarlane
I. D. Mcfarlane
Joan M. Mackie
Rita J. McLaughlin
D. McMillan
P. I. Maguire
Doris Mangan
V. Martin
Sheila M. Mason
W. R. Matthews
H. H. Meinhard
Douglas Miller
Helen M. Mitchell
W. H. Mittins
W. G. Moore
J. Morgan
Thelma Morris

D. J. Mossop
G. Muller
Robert A. Murphy
V. G. Mylne

R. Niklaus
J. S. Nockels

Anne Page
Sr. Pauline
B. Peace
M. Pénillault
Sr. Mary Peter
J. W. Petrie
M. Celia Phillips
D. Place
Gillian A. Post
D. C. Potts
A. R. Pugh

Elizabeth Ratcliff
June E. Raynal
I. G. Redding
J. A. Z. Redding
Joselyne Reed
K. S. Reid
Isabel Richmond
V. P. Rimer
N. S. Rinsler
P. E. J. Robinson
Kenneth Rockett
Graham E. Rodmell
Pat Rogers
D. J. Ross
Martin Roth
Margaret A. E. Rowland
Thelma Rushbrooke

F. W. Saunders
B. Saunderson
Doreen Saxe
R. A. Sayce
H. J. M. Scott
Jean Seznec
Robert Shackleton
Marjorie Shaw
Janet Sheldon
Marjorie F. Sherborne
N. D. Shergold
N. G. Sherwood
David J. Shirt
Mary T. Shirt

LIST OF SUBSCRIBERS

Robert F. Sinclair
G. Smart
B. E. Q. Smith
Monica M. Smith
Peter Solan
Dorothy Soulsby
Ian H. Soulsby
Michael C. Sparrow
H. P. Stadler
Susan Stanbrook
Caroline Stanley
A. J. Steele
W. Mc. C. Stewart
F. E. Sutcliffe
H. L. Sutcliffe
J. A. Suttton

L. W. Tancock
Anthony L. Taylor
Elizabeth I. Taylor
J. M. Taylor
O. R. Taylor
Samuel S. B. Taylor
S. W. Taylor
Christopher Thacker
Herbert Thearle
Valerie C. Thomas
P. D. Thompson

Heather M. Tilbrook
Margaret G. Tillet
Susan E. Tither
Lili Todes
Olive G. Tomkeieff
J. P. Tuck

Peter Ure

Norman & Nancy Ward
H. W. Wardman
D. A. Warren
Avril C. Watson
R. Watson
B. Western
G. Wheeler
H. L. Hudson-Williams
D. B. Wilson
Mabel F. Wilson
B. Woledge
Henry Wood
Linda & Leslie Woodhall
M. J. Worthington

P. J. Yarrow
Jozy Yates

Eileen E. Zwalf

LIBRARIES

Aberdeen University
The Queen's University, Belfast
Birmingham University
Cambridge: Gonville & Caius College
          Magdalene College
University College, Dublin
Dundee University
Durham University
University of East Anglia
Hull University
University of Keele
University of Kent at Canterbury
University of Lancaster
Leeds University
Leicester University
London: Birkbeck College
      Royal Holloway College
      University College
      Westfield College
Magee University College
University of Nottingham
Oxford: Oriel College
     Queen's College
     St Anne's College
     St Catherine's College
     Somerville College
     Taylor Institution
Rice University, Houston, Texas
University of St Andrews
Sheffield University
University College of Swansea
University of Warwick

University of Newcastle upon Tyne: the Soirée Française 1968–1969